Traditional Edgings To Crochet

Edited by
RITA WEISS

Dover Publications, Inc., New York

CROCHET ABBREVIATIONS

ch	chain	**sl st**	slip stitch
sc	single crochet	**pc st**	popcorn stitch
half dc	half double crochet	**sp**	space
		st(s)	stitch(es)
dc	double crochet	**rnd**	round
		incl	inclusive
tr	treble	**inc**	increase
d tr	double treble	**dec**	decrease

*(asterisk) or † (dagger) . . . Repeat the instructions following the asterisk or dagger as many times as specified.

** or † † . . . Used for a second set of repeats within one set of instructions.

Repeat instructions in parentheses as many times as specified. For example: "**(Ch 5, sc in next sc) 5 times**" means to make all that is in parentheses 5 times in all.

This Dover edition, first published in 1987, is a new selection of patterns from *Star Book of 100 Edgings: Crocheted, Tatted, Knitted. Book 18,* published by the American Thread Company, New York, in 1942; *Edgings for All Purposes Including Church Laces, Book No. 320,* published by Coats & Clark, Inc., New York, in 1956; *Decorating with Crochet, Direction Book 1800,* published by the Lily Mills Co., Shelby, N.C., in 1948; *Crochet and Tatting, Heirloom Edition, Star Book No. 66,* published by the American Thread Company in 1949; *Floral Insertions and Floral Edgings, Book No. 263,* published by The Spool Cotton Company, New York, in 1949; *Handkerchief Edgings, Book No. 311,* published by Coats & Clark, Inc., in 1955; and *Edgings, Book No. 8,* published by Royal Society, Inc., in 1947. A new introduction has been specially written for this edition.

Manufactured in the United States of America
Dover Publications, Inc., 31 East 2nd Street, Mineola, N.Y. 11501

Library of Congress Cataloging-in-Publication Data

Traditional edgings to crochet.

(Dover needlework series)
Reprinted from thread-company leaflets originally published 1942–1956.
1. Crocheting—Patterns. I. Weiss, Rita. II. Series.
TT825.T73 1986   746.43′4041   86-19637
ISBN 0-486-25238-8 (pbk.)

Introduction

For years crocheters have been fascinated with crocheted edgings. If they had no time to make a tablecloth or even a doily, they could still personalize any item by simply adding a handmade crocheted edging.

This collection contains some of the best crocheted edging patterns that have appeared in instructional booklets published by America's thread companies during the first part of this century. During that period, hundreds of instructional booklets were created as a device for selling more thread. Among the most popular of the patterns published were those for crocheted edgings. Many of these old instructional booklets and the edgings they inspired have now become collector's items. Modern technology permits us to show the patterns to you exactly as they originally appeared.

Many of the patterns make no suggestion for thread or hook size since the size of the thread determines the width and texture of the edging; very fine threads create finer lace while coarser threads produce heavier edgings. Page 46 shows the same edging pattern worked in various weights of thread and suggests the proper hook for each thread. Finer threads require a finer hook; a heavier hook is used with heavier threads. You may want to experiment with different weights of thread and sizes of hooks to determine your favorite lace.

Edgings that are crocheted the *long way* are worked on a foundation chain or directly on the fabric. Those worked on a foundation chain can be cut, if necessary, to obtain the desired length. Cut at the end of the complete pattern; fasten the loose threads at the ends of rows, and hem or overcast the cut edge.

Edgings crocheted the *short way* are easier to do than those crocheted the long way because they can be worked to the exact length required.

When you have completed your edging, wash and block it. Wash in warm water with a good neutral soap or detergent, squeezing the suds through the work. Rinse in clear water. Starching the edging will give it a crisper look and add body. Using rustproof pins, pin the edging right side down on a well-padded surface. Be sure to pin out all picots, loops, scallops, etc. When the edging is almost completely dry, press through a damp cloth with a moderately hot iron. Do not rest the iron on the decorative, raised stitches! When thoroughly dry, remove the pins.

The crochet terminology and hooks listed in this book are those used in the United States. The following charts give the U.S. name of crochet stitches and their equivalent in other countries and the equivalents to U.S. crochet hook sizes. Crocheters should become thoroughly familiar with the differences in both crochet terms and hook sizes before starting any project.

All of the stitches used in the edgings in this book are explained on page 47.

STITCH CONVERSION CHART

U.S. Name	Equivalent
Chain	Chain
Slip	Single crochet
Single crochet	Double crochet
Half-double or short-double crochet	Half-treble crochet
Double crochet	Treble crochet
Treble crochet	Double-treble crochet
Double-treble crochet	Treble-treble crochet
Treble-treble or long-treble crochet	Quadruple-treble crochet
Afghan stitch	Tricot crochet

HOOK CONVERSION CHART

Aluminum

U.S. Size	B	C	D	E	F	G	H	I	J	K
British & Canadian Size	12	11	10	9	8	7	5	4	3	2
Metric Size	2½	3	—	3½	4	4½	5	5½	6	7

Steel

U.S. Size	00	0	1	2	3	4	5	6
British & Canadian Size	000	00	0	1	—	1½	2	2½

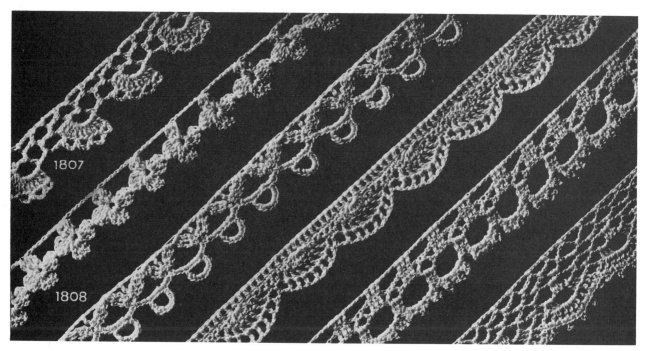

1807   1808   1809   1810   1811   1812

Delicate Edgings...

Materials Suggested — AMERICAN THREAD COMPANY
"STAR" or "GEM" MERCERIZED CROCHET COTTON
Sizes 30 to 70 or "STAR" TATTING COTTON

No. 1807

Ch 11, d c in 7th st from hook, ch 3, skip 3 chs, d c in end ch, ch 6, turn.

2nd Row. D c in 1st mesh, ch 3, d c in next mesh, ch 5, turn.

3rd Row. D c in 1st mesh, ch 3, 10 d c in next mesh, d c in next mesh, ch 3, turn.

4th Row. S c in next d c, * ch 3, skip 1 d c, s c in next d c, repeat from * twice, ch 4, d c in next mesh, ch 3, d c in end mesh, ch 5, turn.

5th Row. D c in 1st mesh, ch 3, d c in next mesh, ch 6, turn.

6th Row. D c in 1st mesh, ch 3, d c in next mesh, ch 5, turn.

7th Row. D c in 1st mesh, ch 3, 10 d c in next mesh, d c in next mesh, ch 3, turn and repeat from 4th row for length desired.

No. 1808

Ch 5, d c in 1st ch, ch 3, 2 d c in top of d c just made, ch 3, sl st in same space, * ch 3, 2 d c in same space, ch 3, sl st in same space, repeat from *, d c in 1st ch, ch 3, s c in same space, ** ch 11, d c in 5th st from hook, ch 3, d c in top of d c just made, sl st in side petal of 1st clover, d c in same space, ch 3, sl st in same space and complete clover same as 1st clover, repeat from ** for length desired.

No. 1809

Chain somewhat longer than required. A cluster in 6th chain (thread over 3 times, insert in 6th chain, draw through 2 loops 3 times, thread over 3 times, draw up a loop, draw through 2 loops 3 times, then through all loops on hook), * chain 7—3 d tr cluster in same st with cluster just made, leaving last 4 loops on hook; thread over twice, skip 2 chs, insert in next chain, draw through 2 loops twice, then through all loops on hook, skip 2 chs, 3 d tr cluster in next chain st and repeat from * to end of row. Turn.

2nd Row. 7 s c over 7 chain loop, ch 7, turn, skip 3 s c, sl st in next s c, ch 1, turn and work 9 s c over loop just made, 3 s c over first chain loop, repeat to end of row.

No. 1810

Work a ch for length desired, 1 d c in 4th st from hook, 1 d c in each remaining ch, turn.

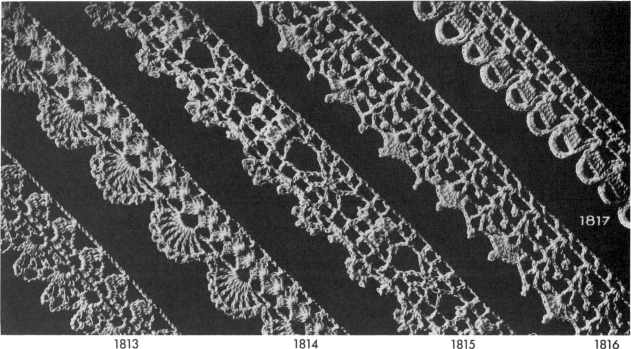

1817

1813   1814   1815   1816

For a Fine Finish

2nd Row. * 1 s c in each of the next 5 d c, skip 2 d c, 7 d c in next d c, skip 2 d c, repeat from * across row, turn.

3rd Row. 1 s c in each of the 3 center s c, ch 1, 1 d c in each d c with ch 1 between, ch 1, repeat from beginning across row, turn.

4th Row. 1 s c in center s c, ch 1, 1 d c with ch 2 between in each d c, ch 1, repeat from beginning across row, break thread.

No. 1811

Ch for desired length, d c in 4th st of ch, 1 d c in each of the next 2 sts, * ch 5, skip 3 sts, 1 d c in each of the next 3 sts, repeat from * across row.

2nd Row. Ch 3, 1 d c in each of the next 2 d c, * d c in center st of ch 5, ch 3, d c in same space, 1 d c in each of the next 3 d c, repeat from * across row.

3rd Row. Starting in 3 ch loop, ch 3, 2 d c in same space, * ch 5, 3 d c in center st of next 3 ch loop, repeat from * across row.

4th Row. Over each 5 ch loop work 2 s c, 4 ch picot, 2 s c, picot, 2 s c, picot, 2 s c.

No. 1812

1st Row. Work a ch as long as desired * ch 5, skip 3 ch, s c in next st, repeat from * across row.

2nd Row. Ch 5, s c in loop, * ch 5, s c in next loop, repeat from * across row.

3rd Row. Repeat 2nd row.

4th Row. * Ch 5, s c in next loop, repeat from *, ** ch 3, 3 d c in next loop, ch 3, s c in next loop, ch 5, s c in next loop, repeat from ** across row.

5th Row. Ch 3, s c in loop, * ch 3, 3 d c in 3 ch loop, ch 5, skip 3 d c of previous row, 3 d c in next loop, ch 3, s c in next loop and repeat from * across row.

6th Row. 1 d c with ch 1 between in each of the next 3 d c, * skip the 2 three ch loops, 1 d c with ch 1 between in each of the next 3 d c, 5 d c with ch 1 between in 5 ch loop, 1 d c with ch 1 between in each of the next 3 d c, repeat from * across row.

7th Row. Work a row of s c and picots.

Instructions for Nos. 1813 to 1817 illustrated above on page 26

Handkerchief Edgings

⟦ S-671 ⟧

COATS & CLARK'S O.N.T. TATTING-CRO-CHET, Art. C.21, Size 70: 1 ball each of No. 1 White and No. 8 Blue.

Milwards Steel Crochet Hook No. 14.

A hairpin lace staple, 1/4 inch wide . . . A rolled edge handkerchief, 11¼ inches square.

With White make a strip of hairpin lace slightly longer than outer edge of handkerchief, allowing for corners. Break off. Sew together at center of hairpin lace, being careful not to twist.

HEADING . . . Keeping the twist in all loops, attach Blue to any loop, sc in same place, * ch 1, sc in next loop. Repeat from * until piece reaches across side.

To form corner: (Ch 1, sc through next 2 loops) 5 times; ch 1, sc in next loop and complete other sides and corners the same way. Join and break off.

SCALLOPED EDGE . . . 1st rnd: Still keeping the twist in all loops, attach Blue to first 2 loops at opposite side of hairpin lace, sc in same place, * draw loop on hook out to measure ⅛ inch, thread over and draw thread through, insert hook between single and double loops and draw thread through, thread over and draw through all loops on hook (knot st made), sc through next 2 loops. Repeat from * around. Join and break off. **2nd rnd:** Attach White to first sc, sc in same place, * make a knot st, sc in next sc. Repeat from * around. Join and break off. **3rd rnd:** Attach Blue to first sc and repeat 2nd rnd. Join and break off. Sew Edging to handkerchief.

⟦ S-672 ⟧

COATS & CLARK'S O.N.T. TATTING-CRO-CHET, Art. C.21, Size 70: 1 ball of No. 1 White.

Milwards Steel Crochet Hook No. 14.

A rolled edge handkerchief, 11½ inches square.

1st rnd: Attach thread to any corner of handkerchief, 4 sc in same place, sc closely around (18 sc to 1 inch), making 4 sc in each corner. Join. **2nd rnd:** In same place as sl st make sc, ch 3 and sc; (ch 7, in next sc make sc, ch 3 and sc) 3 times; * ch 7, skip 5 sc, in next sc make sc, ch 3 and sc. Repeat from * across to within 5 sc of next corner group, ending with ch 7, skip 5 sc, (in next sc make sc, ch 3 and sc, ch 7) 4 times. Complete other sides and corners the same way, ending with

ch 3, tr in first sc. **3rd to 7th rnds incl:** In loop just formed make sc, ch 3 and sc; * ch 7, in next ch-7 loop make sc, ch 3 and sc. Repeat from * around. Join as before. At end of 7th rnd, ch 7, sl st in first sc. Break off.

⟦ S-673 ⟧

COATS & CLARK'S O.N.T. TATTING-CRO-CHET, Art. C.21, Size 70: 1 ball of No. 18-A Shaded Lavenders.

Milwards Steel Crochet Hook No. 14.

A rolled edge handkerchief, 11½ inches square.

Make a chain to reach around handkerchief, allowing 1 inch for each corner. Join, being careful not to twist. **1st rnd:** Ch 3, * draw loop on hook out to measure ⅜ inch, thread over and draw thread through, insert hook between single and double loops and draw loop through, thread over and draw through both loops on hook (knot st made), skip 2 ch, dc in next ch. Repeat from * until piece reaches across side.

To form corner: (Make a knot st, skip 1 ch, dc in next ch) 5 times; make a knot st, skip 2 ch, dc in next ch and complete other sides and corners the same way, having an even number of sps on rnd. Join to top of ch-3. **2nd rnd:** Ch 3, * make a knot st, dc in next dc. Repeat from * around, ending with a knot st. Join. **3rd rnd:** Sc in same place as sl st, * ch 5, sc in next dc, ch 7, sc in 4th ch from hook (picot made), (ch 4, sc in 4th ch from hook) twice (2 more picots made), dc at base of first picot, ch 3, sc in next dc. Repeat from * around. Join and break off. Sew Edging to handkerchief.

⟦ S-674 ⟧

COATS & CLARK'S O.N.T. TATTING-CRO-CHET, Art. C.21, Size 70: 1 ball each of No. 1 White and No. 126 Spanish Red.

Milwards Steel Crochet Hook No. 14.

A rolled edge handkerchief, 11 inches square.

HEART MOTIF . . . Starting at top with Spanish Red, ch 12. Join with sl st to form ring. **1st row:** Ch 3, in ring make dc, ch 2 and 2 dc (shell made), ch 3, 30 tr, ch 3, 2 dc, ch 2 and 2 dc (another shell made). Ch 5, turn. **2nd row:** In first ch-2 sp make 2 dc, ch 2 and 2 dc (shell made over shell);

ch 4, (tr in next tr, ch 1) 29 times; tr in next tr, ch 4, shell in sp of next shell. Ch 5, turn. **3rd row:** Shell over first shell, ch 4, (sc in next ch-1 sp, ch 3) 28 times; sc in next sp, ch 4, shell over shell. Ch 5, turn. **4th row:** Shell over shell, ch 4, (sc in next ch-3 loop, ch 3) 27 times; sc in next loop, ch 4, shell over shell. Ch 5, turn. Continue to work in pattern, having 1 ch-3 loop less on each row until 1 loop remains. Ch 5, turn. **Next row:** Shell over shell, ch 4, sc in ch-3 loop, ch 4, 2 dc in sp of next shell, ch 1, sl st in sp of last shell made, ch 1, 2 dc in same sp as last 2 dc. Break off.

EDGING . . . Attach White to ring, ch 3 and, working around Heart, sc in end dc of first shell, * ch 3, in next ch-5 loop make (sc, ch 3) twice; skip 1 free dc of shell, sc in next dc, ch 3, sc in end dc of next shell. Repeat from * to point of Heart, ending with sc in sl st, ch 3, sc in end dc of next shell and complete other sides to correspond, sl st in ring. Break off.

ROSETTE . . . Starting at center with Red, ch 6. Join with sl st to form ring. **1st rnd:** Ch 6, (dc in ring, ch 3) 5 times. Join to 3rd ch of ch-6. **2nd rnd:** In each sp around make half dc, 3 dc, half dc and sc. Join. **3rd rnd:** * Ch 4, sc in back of first sc on next petal. Repeat from * around. Join. **4th rnd:** In each sp around make sc, half dc, 5 dc, half dc and sc. Join. **5th rnd:** Repeat 3rd rnd. **6th rnd:** In each sp around make half dc, dc, 7 tr, dc and half dc. Join and break off.

TRIM . . . Attach White to first st on any petal on 2nd petal rnd, sc in same place, * ch 3, sc in next st. Repeat from * across petal, ending with sc in last st, sc in first st on next petal. Complete all petals the same way. Join and break off. Work around last rnd of petals the same way.

EDGING . . . **1st rnd:** Attach White to any corner of handkerchief, in same place make sc, ch 5 and sc; * ch 5, skip ¼ inch on handkerchief, sc on edge. Repeat from * around, making sc, ch 5 and sc in each corner and ending with ch 2, dc in first sc. **2nd and 3rd rnds:** * Ch 5, sc in next loop. Repeat from * around, ending with ch 2, sc in dc. Break off at end of 3rd rnd. **4th rnd:** Attach Red to any loop, sc in same place, * ch 5, sc in next loop. Repeat from * around. Join and break off. Sew Heart and Rosette in place.

Directions for Edgings S-675 and S-676 on Page 25. →

S-672

S-671

S-673

S-674

S-675

S-676

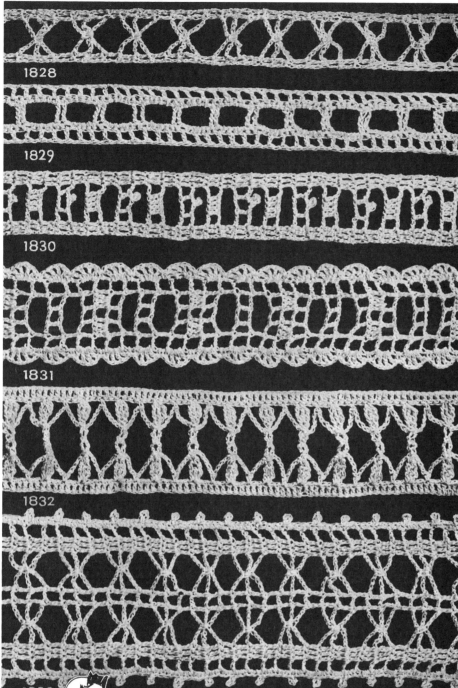

1828

1829

1830

1831

1832

1833

Instructions for Nos. 1830 to 1833 illustrated above on page 26

Beading Is in Fashion

Dresses
Lingerie
Dressing Table Skirts
Bedroom Curtains
Boudoir Pillows
Picture Frames
Bassinettes

Materials Suggested —
AMERICAN THREAD COMPANY
"STAR" or "GEM" MERCERIZED
CROCHET COTTON
Sizes 20 to 70

No. 1828

Ch 15, d c in 4th st from hook, ch 9, skip 9 sts, 1 d c in each of the last 2 sts, ch 3, turn.

2nd Row. D c in d c, ch 4, s c over the two 9 ch loops, ch 4, 1 d c in d c and 1 d c in end ch, ch 3, turn.

***3rd and 4th Rows.** D c in d c, ch 9, 1 d c in d c and 1 d c in end ch, ch 3, turn. Repeat 2nd row and repeat from * for length desired.

No. 1829

Make a ch a trifle longer than desired, tr c in 5th st from hook, * ch 4, skip 4 sts, 1 tr c in each of the next 2 sts, repeat from * to end of ch or length desired. (Cut off remainder of ch) ch 1, turn.

2nd Row. 1 s c in each tr c and 4 s c over each loop, ch 4, turn.

3rd Row. Skip 1 s c, d c over next s c, ch 1 and repeat from beginning. Repeat 2nd and 3rd rows on other side of beading.

Narcissus Vanity Set

MATERIALS:

J. & P. Coats Tatting-Crochet, Size 70, 7 balls of White (No. 1) and 2 balls of Dark Yellow (No. 43) and Hunter's Green (No. 48) . . . ½ yard of yellow organdie . . . Steel Crochet Hook No. 14.

Centerpiece measures 11½ x 17 inches; each side piece measures 10 inches square.

FIRST NARCISSUS . . . Starting at center with White, ch 6. Join with sl st to form ring.

FIRST PETAL . . . 1st row: Ch 3, 3 dc in ring. Ch 3, turn. **2nd row:** Dc in first dc, 2 dc in next 2 dc, 2 dc in top of turning chain. Ch 3, turn. **3rd row:** Skip first dc, holding back on hook the last loop of each dc, make dc in next 3 dc, thread over and draw through all loops on hook (2 dc decreased), dc in next dc, work off next 3 sts as 1 dc. Ch 3, turn. **4th row:** Skip first dc, work off all other sts as 1 st. Break off.

SECOND PETAL . . . Attach White to ring, ch 3 and complete as for First Petal.

Make 4 more petals in this manner.

CENTER . . . Starting at base with Dark Yellow, ch 4. **1st rnd:** 7 dc in 4th ch from hook, sl st in top of starting chain. **2nd rnd:** Ch 3, dc in same place as sl st, dc in next 2 dc, 2 dc in next dc (1 dc increased), dc in next 3 dc. Join. **3rd rnd:** Ch 3, dc in each dc, increasing 1 dc at opposite points of rnd. **4th rnd:** Sc in same place as sl st, * ch 5, sc in next dc. Repeat from * around, ending with ch 5, sl st in first sc. Break off. Sew Center in place.

Make 40 flowers for centerpiece and 28 flowers for each side piece.

For Centerpiece, tack 7 flowers together at 2 opposite points, leaving 2 petals free on each side of joining for each short side. Join 11 flowers in same manner for each long side. To form corner, join a flower to end flowers of 2 adjacent sides, leaving 4 petals free on outer edge on corner flower.

For each side piece join 6 flowers for each side and one at each corner as before.

HEADING . . . Attach Green to point of first free petal on inner edge of long side, sc in same place, * ch 6, sc in tip of next petal, ch 6, skip 2 rows of next petal, make a long tr in end st of next row—*to make a long tr, thread over hook 5 times*—skip cluster on next petal, make a long tr in end st of next row, ch 6, sc in tip of next petal. Repeat from * across to corner, ending with sc.

To Form Corner: Ch 4, (make a long tr in joining of next 2 petals) twice; ch 4, sc in tip of next petal, and work as for other side. Complete rnd, making corners as before. Join and break off.

Cut 3 pieces of organdie, each slightly larger all around than inner edge of corresponding crocheted edgings. Make a narrow hem around each piece. Sew Edgings in place.

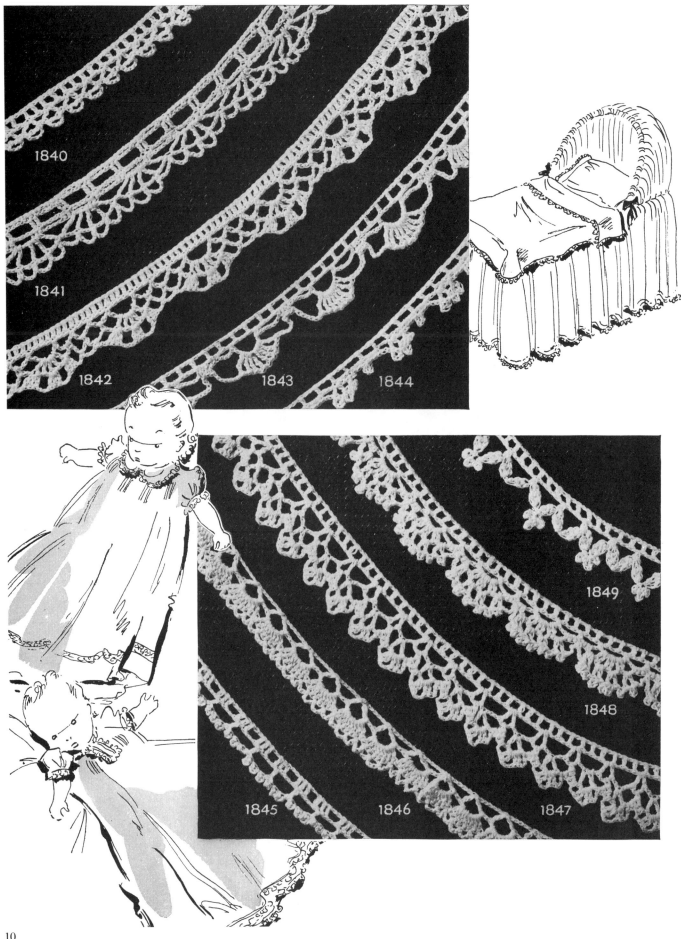

1840

1841

1842

1843

1844

1845

1846

1847

1848

1849

Edgings for Babies

DAINTY AS DANCING SNOWFLAKES

Materials Suggested — AMERICAN THREAD COMPANY "STAR" TATTING COTTON or "STAR" or "GEM" MERCERIZED CROCHET COTTON Sizes 50 to 70

No. 1840

Ch for desired length, 1 d c in 5th st from hook, * ch 1, skip 1 ch, d c in next ch, repeat from * across row, turn.

2nd Row. Ch 3, d c in next d c, * ch 5, d c in top of d c just made, d c in same space with 1st d c of shell, skip 1 d c, d c in next d c, repeat from * across row.

No. 1841

Ch for desired length, turn 1 s c in 2nd st from hook, * ch 4, skip 4 chs, 1 s c in each of the next 2 chs, repeat from * ch 3, turn.

2nd Row. 1 d c in s c, * ch 4, 1 d c in each of the next 2 s c, repeat from * ch 1, turn.

3rd Row. S c in d c, * ch 4, 1 s c in each d c, repeat from *.

4th Row. Sl st into loop, ch 6, 4 tr c with ch 2 between in same loop, * skip 1 loop, 5 tr c with ch 2 between in next loop, repeat from *.

5th Row. Ch 5, s c in next tr c, repeat from beginning across row.

No. 1842

Work a ch for desired length, d c in 4th st from hook, 1 d c in each remaining ch, turn.

2nd Row. * ch 5, skip 2 d c, sl st in next d c, repeat from * twice, ch 7, skip 3 d c, sl st in next d c, repeat from beginning across row ending with the 3 small loops, turn.

3rd Row. Sl st to center of loop, * ch 5, s c in next loop, repeat from *, ch 2, ** 5 d c with ch 1 between in next loop, ch 2, s c in next loop, * ch 5, s c in next loop, repeat from *, ch 2, repeat from ** across row, turn.

4th Row. S c in loop, ch 3, s c in next loop, ch 2, ** 3 d c in 1st d c, * ch 3, skip 1 d c, 3 d c in next d c, repeat from *, ch 2, s c in next loop, ch 3, s c in next loop, ch 2, repeat from ** across row. Break thread.

No. 1843

Ch for desired length, d c in 8th st from hook, * ch 2, skip 2 sts, d c in next st, repeat from * for length desired, ch 1, turn.

2nd Row. 3 s c in mesh, * ch 7, skip 1 mesh, s c in next mesh, ch 7, skip 1 mesh, s c in next mesh, ch 7, skip 1 mesh, 3 s c in next mesh, repeat from * across row ending with 3 s c, ch 1, turn.

3rd Row. * 1 s c in each s c, ch 7, skip 1 loop, 8 tr c with ch 1 between in next loop, ch 7, repeat from * across row.

No. 1844

Ch for desired length, d c in 8th st from hook, * ch 2, skip 2 sts, d c in next st, repeat from * for entire length.

2nd Row. Ch 1, work 3 s c in 1st mesh, ch 4, sl st in 4th st from hook for picot, ** 3 s c in next mesh, ch 2, skip 1 d c, d c in next d c, * 4 ch picot, d c in same space, repeat from *, picot, ch 2, skip 1 mesh, 3 s c in next mesh, picot, repeat from ** across row.

No. 1845

Ch for desired length, d c in 4th st from hook, 1 d c in next ch, * ch 2, skip 2 chs, 1 d c in each of the next 3 chs, repeat from * across row, turn.

2nd Row. Sl st to next d c, ch 7, sl st in 4th st from hook for picot, * ch 4, sl st in 1st ch for picot, repeat from *, d c in center d c of next group and repeat across row.

No. 1846

Ch for desired length, d c in 4th st from needle, * ch 5, d c in same space, ch 2, skip 5 chs, d c in next ch, repeat from * across row, ch 5, d c in same space, turn.

2nd Row. Ch 3 and work 7 d c in 1st loop, * skip the ch 2, 8 d c in next loop, repeat from * across row, turn.

3rd Row. * Ch 4, skip 1 d c, sl st in next d c, repeat from * across row.

No. 1847

Ch for desired length, d c in 5th st from hook, * ch 1, skip 1 st, d c in next st, repeat from * across row, turn.

2nd Row. Sl st into mesh, ch 6, d c in same space, * ch 5, skip 2 meshes, 2 d c with ch 3 between in next mesh, repeat from * across row, turn.

3rd Row. Sl st to center of 3 ch loop, * ch 3, d c in center st of next ch, ch 3, d c in same space, ch 3, s c in next 3 ch loop, repeat from * across row, turn.

4th Row. 2 s c over 1st loop, * ch 2, 2 d c in next loop, ch 3, 2 d c in same loop, ch 2, 2 s c over each of the next 2 loops, repeat from * across row.

No. 1848

Ch for desired length, d c in 5th st from hook, * ch 1, skip 1 st, d c in next st, repeat from * across row, turn.

2nd Row. Sl st to mesh, * ch 5, skip 1 mesh, s c in next mesh, repeat from * across row, turn.

3rd Row. 3 s c over each of the 1st 2 loops, ch 2, 2 d c in next loop, * ch 2, 2 d c in same loop and repeat from *, ch 2, repeat from beginning, turn.

4th Row. Sl st to center of group of s c, ch 3, * d c in next 2 ch loop, ch 4, sl st in 4th st from hook for picot, d c in same loop, ch 4, sl st in 4th st from hook for picot, repeat from * twice, d c in next 2 ch loop, ch 4, sl st in 4th st for picot, d c in same loop, ch 3, sl st in center of next group of s c and continue across row.

No. 1849

Ch for desired length, d c in 5th st from hook, * ch 1, skip 1 ch, d c in next ch, repeat from * across row, turn.

2nd Row. Ch 4, thread over needle, insert in 1 st ch and work off 2 loops, thread over needle, insert in same space and work off all loops 2 at a time, ch 4, thread over needle, insert in 1 st ch and work off 2 loops, thread over needle insert in same space and work off all loops 2 at a time, skip 1 d c, s c in next d c, 1 cluster st, ch 4, sl st in 1st ch for picot, * ch 4, sl st in same space for picot, repeat from *, ch 4 thread over needle, insert in 1st ch and work off 2 loops, thread over needle, insert in same space and work off all loops 2 at a time, skip 2 d c, s c in next d c, repeat from beginning across row.

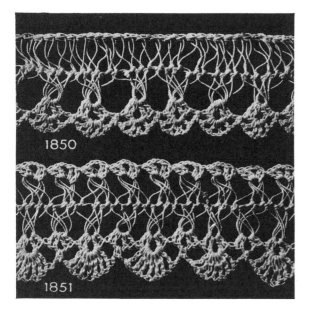

1850

1851

Old-Fashioned Hairpin Lace Edgings

The distinctive charm of hairpin lace is revived in these graceful *new* patterns—so easy to make.

Materials Suggested — AMERICAN THREAD COMPANY "STAR" or "GEM" MERCERIZED CROCHET COTTON Sizes 10 to 70

HAIRPIN LACE

Hairpin lace staple and a crochet hook are required.

Make a loose ch on hook, drop loop off hook and insert the left hand prong of staple upwards into loop. Draw loop until the knot is in the center between the prongs. Bring the thread in front around the right hand prong and insert hook in loop around the left hand prong drawing the thread through and making a ch st. * Do not draw out the loop on hook, turn the hook upwards so it parallels the prongs, pass it between the prongs to the back of the staple. Turn the staple over to the left (making a loop over right prong). Insert crochet hook up through the front thread of loop at left and work an s c. Repeat from * until prongs are filled with loops, slip loops off, replace prongs into the last 4 loops and continue work for desired length.

No. 1850

Work Hairpin lace for length desired. In crocheting keep the twist in the loops. Across one side work an s c in each loop.

Scallop. **1st Row.** Join thread in first 4 loops, ch 3, 1 d c over loops, ch 3, 2 d c in same space, * 2 d c over next 4 loops, ch 3, 2 d c in same space, repeat from * across row.

2nd Row. S c between shells, ch 2, 4 d c with ch 2 between in next shell, ch 2, repeat from beginning across row.

No. 1851

Edging. Work a length of Hairpin lace.

Join thread in 3 loops of lace, ch 2, d c in same space, ch 2, 2 d c in same space, * 2 d c in next 3 loops, ch 2, d c in same space, repeat from * across length.

2nd Row. S c in 1st shell, * ch 2, 7 tr c with ch 1 between in next shell, ch 2, s c in next shell, repeat from * across length, break thread and repeat 1st row on other side of edging.

No. 1852

Work a length of Hairpin lace. Join thread in 3 loops of lace and work 1 s c, * ch 3, s c over next 3 loops, repeat from * across length and repeat on other side of lace. Scallop. Sl st into loop, ch 3, * thread over, insert in loop and work off 2 loops, repeat from * and work off all loops 2 at a time ** ch 6, * thread over, insert in next loop and work off 2 loops, repeat from * twice and work off remaining loops 2 at a time, repeat from ** across length.

No. 1853

Work a length of Hairpin lace and repeat the 1st row of edging No. 1851 on both sides of Hairpin lace.

No. 1854

Work a length of Hairpin lace.

Join thread over 2 loops of lace and work 1 s c, * ch 1, s c over next 2 loops, repeat from * across side.

2nd Row. Ch 3, d c in s c, ch 4, d c in top of d c just made, d c in same s c with last d c, ch 4, d c in top of d c just made, * skip 1 s c, d c in next d c, ch 4, d c in top of last d c made, d c in same s c with last d c, ch 4, d c in top of d c just made and repeat from * across row.

Repeat the 1st row on other side of edging.

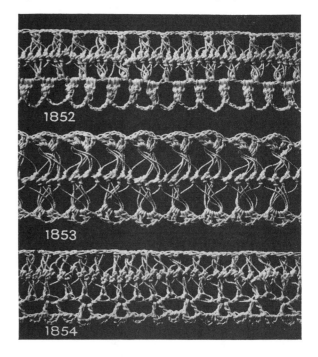

1852

1853

1854

Towel Edgings

MATERIALS—DAISY Mercerized Crochet Cotton in Unbleached and a color. No. 5 hook.

WIDE EDGING—Motif—With color, ch 6, making 1st st about twice usual length, 1 dc in long st, (ch 1, 1 dc in long st) 10 times, ch 1, 1 sl st in 2d ch st from 1st dc. **ROW 2**—* Ch 16, marking 9th st with a pin, remove hook, insert in 1st st of ch, catch loop and pull thru, ch 1, (2 sc, 2 hdc and 5 dc) over half of ch, * (3 dc, a 4-ch p in last dc, and 3 dc) in marked st, (5 dc, 2 hdc and 2 sc) over balance of ch, 1 sl st in ch st at base of loop, ** 1 sc over next 1-ch of center circle, 1 sc in dc, 1 sc over next 1-ch. Repeat from * to *. Then ch 4, remove hook. insert in 9th st up side of previous petal, catch loop and pull thru, (3 sc, a 4-ch p and 2 sc) over 4-ch, 1 sl st in last dc. Repeat from last * to **

to complete another petal, 1 sc in next dc, 1 sc over 1-ch, 1 sc in dc. Now make and join another petal. Then, 1 sc over 1-ch, 1 sc in dc, 1 sc over 1-ch. Make another petal, then, 1 sc in dc, 1 sc over 1-ch, 1 sc in dc. Make another petal. Then, * 1 sc over 1-ch, 1 sc in dc, 1 sc over 1-ch, a p, 1 sc in dc, 1 sc over 1-ch, * 1 sc in dc, a p. Repeat from * to *, 1 sl st in starting st. Fasten off. Make another Motif as far as the p at tip of 5th petal. In place of p, ch 7, 1 sl st in p at tip of 1st petal of 1st Motif, ch 4, sk last 4 sts of 7-ch, 1 sl st in next, ch 2, 1 sl st in top of last dc. Complete Motif. Make and join 4 more Motifs in same way.

HEADING ROWS—Join Unbleached to p at tip of 5th petal of Motif at right-hand end of lace, ch 16, sk 5 dc across top of Motif, 1 sc in next dc, * ch 6, 1 sc in 5th st from hook to form a 5-ch p, ch 2, 1 tr in next p on Motif, ch 5, 1 sc in 1st st of 5-ch to form a p, ch 1, 1 tr in next p, (a ch-5 p, ch 1, 1 tr in same p) 4 times, a ch-5 p, ch 1, 1 tr in next p, ch 6, p, ch 2, sk 6 sts on next petal, 1 sc in next, ** a ch-5 p, ch 1, 1 dtr under top 4-ch connecting Motifs, (a ch-5 p, ch 1, 1 dtr in same place) 3 times, a ch-5 p, ch 1, sk 5 dc of next petal, 1 sc in next. Repeat from * 4 times, then repeat from * to ** once. Ch 16, 1 sc in p at end of same petal. Fasten off. **ROW 2**—Join Unbleached to 8th st of 16-ch at start of last row, ch 10, 1 dtr in next 2d st of same 16-ch, * ch 2, 1 dtr in next tr, ch 3, 1 dtr in next tr, ch 3, 1 tr in next tr, ch 4, 1 dc in next tr, ch 4, 1 tr in next tr, (ch 3, 1 dtr in next tr) twice, ** ch 2, 1 dtr in next dtr, (ch 3, 1 dtr in next dtr) 3 times. Repeat from * 4 times and from * to ** once. Ch 2, 1 dtr in 7th st of end 8-ch, ch 3, 1 dtr in next 2d st of same ch. Fasten off. **ROW 3**—Join color to p where 1st Heading Row started, ch 1, 8 sc over next 8-ch, 1 sc in next st, 6 sc over next ch, 1 sl st in 7th st of same 10-ch, ch 3, 1 dc in same st, 3 dc over balance of same ch, 1 dc in dtr, * 2 dc over 2-ch, 1 dc in dtr, (3 dc over 3-ch, 1 dc in next st) twice, (4 dc over 4-ch, 1 dc in next st) twice, (3 dc over 3-ch, 1 dc in next st) twice, 2 dc over 2-ch, 1 dc in next st, ** (3 dc over 3-ch, 1 dc in next st) 3 times. Repeat from * 4 times and from * to ** once. 3 dc over next 3-ch, 1 dc in dtr, ch 3, 1 sl st in same st, 6 sc over dtr, 1 sc in next st, 8 sc over next 8-ch, 1 sl st in p. Fasten off. **ROW 4**—Join Unbleached to 1st dc of last row, ch 5, 1 dc in next 3d dc, (ch 2, 1 dc in next 3d dc) repeated across and fasten off.

NARROW EDGING—Motif—With color, ch 7, join with a sl st into a ring. 10 sc over ring, 1 sl st in back loop of 1st sc, * ch 10, marking 6th st with a pin, remove hook, insert in 1st st of 10-ch, catch loop and pull thru, ch 1, (2 sc, 1 hdc and 2 dc) over half of loop, ** (3 dc, a 4-ch p in last dc, and 3 dc) in marked st, (2 dc, 1 hdc and 2 sc) over balance of loop, 1 sl st in st at base of loop, 1 sl st in back loop of next sc on ring. Repeat from * to **. Ch 2, 1 sl st across in 5th st up side of previous petal, (2 sc, a 4-ch p, and 1 sc) over 2-ch, 1 sl st in top of last dc. Repeat from ** until 5 petals are completed. 1 sl st in back loops of next 3 sc on ring, ch 4, 1 sl st in same last sc, 1 sl st in remaining 2 sc around ring. Fasten off. Make another Motif as far as the p at tip of 5th petal. In place of p, ch 4, 1 sl st in p at tip of 1st petal of previous Motif, ch 2, sk last 2 sts of 4-ch, 1 sl st in next, ch 2, 1 sl st in last dc. Now complete Motif. Make and join 9 Motifs altogether. **Heading Rows**—Join Unbleached to p at tip of 5th petal of end Motif, ch 12, 1 tr in 4th dc around top of same petal, * ch 2, 1 dtr in 4-ch p at center-top of Motif, ch 3, 1 tr in same p, ch 3, 1 dtr in same p, ch 2, 1 tr in 5th st of next petal, ** ch 2, 1 dtr under top half of 2-ch loop connecting Motifs, ch 3, 1 tr in same place, ch 3, 1 dtr in same place, ch 2, 1 tr in 4th dc of next petal. Repeat from * 7 times, and from * to ** once. Ch 12, 1 sc in p at tip of end petal. Fasten off. **ROW 2**—Join color to start of last row, 6 sc over half of 1st 12-ch, 1 sl st in 7th st of same ch, ch 3, 1 dc in same st, 5 dc over balance of 12-ch, 1 dc in tr, 2 dc over 2-ch, 1 dc in dtr, * (3 dc over 3-ch, 1 dc in next st) twice, (2 dc over next 2-ch, 1 dc in next st) twice, (3 dc over 3-ch, 1 dc in next st) twice, (2 dc over 2-ch, 1 dc in next st) twice. Repeat from * across to the 12-ch loop at other end. 5 dc over 12-ch, (1 dc, ch 3, 1 sl st) in 6th st of 12-ch, 6 sc over balance of 12-ch, 1 sl st in p. Fasten off. **ROW 3**—Join Unbleached to top of 3-ch at start of row of dc, ch 5, 1 dc in next 3d dc, (ch 2, 1 dc in next 3d dc) repeated to end of row. Fasten off.

Sew lace to ends of Towel. Stretch and pin lace right-side-down on a padded ironing board, and steam with a hot iron and wet cloth, then press thru a dry cloth until thoroughly **dry**.

Flower Edgings

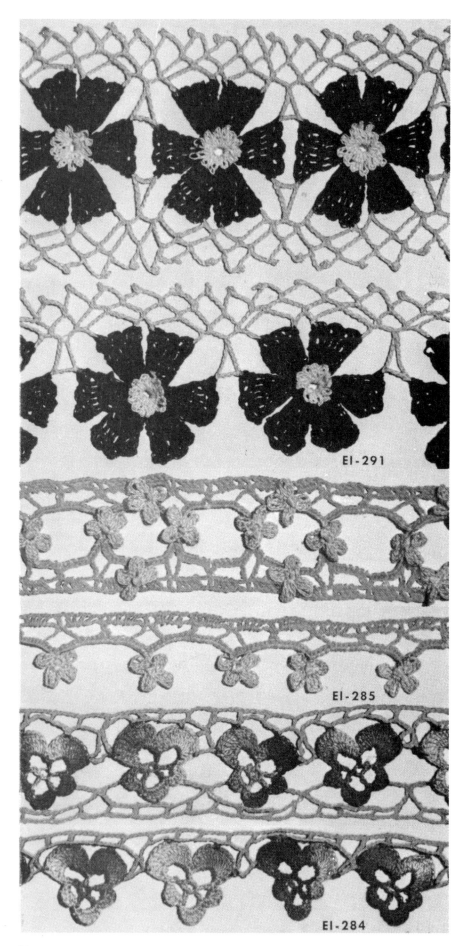

EI-291

EI-285

EI-284

EI 291 ——— Cosmos
← EDGING and INSERTION

MATERIALS:

J. & P. Coats Tatting-Crochet, Size 70, Spanish Red (No. 126), Bright Nile Green (No. 26-B) and Dk. Yellow (No. 43) . . . Steel Crochet Hook No. 14.

EDGING—FIRST FLOWER . . . Starting at center with Red, ch 12. Join with sl st to form ring.

FIRST PETAL . . . 1st row: Ch 3, 4 dc in ring. Ch 3, turn. **2nd row:** Dc in first dc, dc in next 3 dc, 2 dc in top of turning chain. Ch 3, turn. **3rd row:** Skip first dc, dc in each dc across, 2 dc in top of turning chain. Ch 1, turn. **4th row:** (Sc in next dc, ch 1, dc in next dc, ch 1) 3 times; sc in top of turning chain. Break off.

SECOND PETAL . . . Attach Red to ring, ch 3 and complete petal as before. Make 6 more petals in this manner.

CENTER . . . With Yellow, ch 6. Join with sl st to form ring. (Ch 5, sc in ring) 12 times. Break off.

Sew Center in place. Make necessary number of flowers.

HEADING . . . 1st row: Attach Green to last st on any Petal of flower, ch 9, * dc in first st on last row of next petal, ch 9, sc in last st of same row, ch 3, sc in first st on last row of next petal, ch 9, dc in last st on same row, ch 9, sc in first st of last row on next petal, ch 3, sc in last st on any petal on next flower, ch 6, sl st in 3rd ch of ch-9 made, ch 3. Repeat from * across, ending with ch 9, sc in next petal. Turn. **2nd row:** Ch 6, sl st in 6th ch of ch-9, ch 6, sc in same ch-9 loop, * ch 6, sc in next loop. Repeat from * across, ending with sc in last ch-9 loop, ch 6, sc in 6th ch of ch-9 loop. Turn. **3rd row:** Sl st in next 3 ch, * ch 6, sl st in 3rd ch from hook (picot made), ch 3, sc in next loop. Repeat from * across. Break off.

INSERTION . . . Work as for Edging making Heading on both long sides.

EI-284 ——— Pansy
← EDGING and INSERTION

MATERIALS:

J. & P. Coats Tatting-Crochet, Size 70, Shaded Fuchsia (No. 22-C), Shaded Yellows (No. 19), Shaded Lavenders (No. 18) and Hunter's Green (No. 48) . . . Steel Crochet Hook No. 14.

EDGING—FIRST PANSY . . .
Starting at center with Shaded Fuchsia, ch 6. Join with sl st to form ring. **1st rnd:** Ch 6, half dc in ring, ch 7, half dc in ring, ch 5, half dc in ring, ch 9, half dc in ring, ch 9, sl st in 2nd ch of ch-6 first made. **2nd rnd:** In next loop make sc, half dc, 3 dc, half dc and sc (petal); in next loop make sc, half dc, 5 dc, half dc and sc (another petal), in next loop make a petal of sc, half dc, 3 dc, half dc and sc; (in next loop make a large petal of sc, half dc, dc, 11 tr, dc, half dc and sc) twice; sl st in first sc. Break off.

Make 2 more Pansies, one of Shaded Yellows and one of Shaded Lavenders. Make necessary number of Pansies, arranging colors as established.

HEADING . . . 1st row: Attach Green to first tr on first large petal, ch 9, * skip 5 tr, sc in next tr, ch 9, skip 7 sts on next large petal, sc in next tr, ch 10, skip 5 tr on same petal, sc in next tr, ch 4, sc in first tr of next large petal on next pansy, ch 5, sl st in previous ch-10 loop, ch 5. Repeat from * across, ending with ch 5, skip 5 tr on second large petal of last Pansy, tr in next tr. Ch 5, turn. **2nd row:** Dc in next sp, ch 4, dc in next sp, * ch 4, dc in same sp, (ch 4, dc in next sp) 3 times. Repeat from * across. Break off.

INSERTION . . . Work as for Edging No. EI-284 until Heading is completed. Now work Heading on the opposite side as follows: **1st row:** Attach Green to tip of first small petal, * ch 9, sc in tip of next petal, ch 9, tr in tip of next petal, tr in tip of next free petal. Repeat from * across, ending with tr in tip of last free petal of last pansy. Turn. **2nd row:** * Ch 4, in next sp make dc, ch 4 and dc. Repeat from * across. Break off.

EI-285 Forget-Me-Not
EDGING and INSERTION

MATERIALS:

J. & P. Coats Tatting-Crochet, Size 70, Blue (No. 8), and Hunter's Green (No. 48), and

J. & P. Coats or Clark's O.N.T. Six Strand Embroidery Floss, 2 skeins of Yellow (No. 9).

Steel Crochet Hook No. 14.

EDGING—FORGET-ME-NOT . . .
Starting at center of Flower with Blue, ch 1 loosely, ch 4 more in the usual manner. * Holding back on hook the last loop of each tr make 2 tr in 5th ch from hook, thread over and draw through all loops on hook (cluster), ch 4, sl st in same place as last tr was made (petal); ch 4, make a 2-tr cluster in same place as last cluster was made, ch 4, sl st in same place (another petal). Make 2 more petals (Forget-Me-Not completed). Ch 20. Repeat from * until piece measures 1¼ times the length desired. With 3 strands of Six Strand make a French

knot (5 times over needle) in center of each Forget-Me-Not.

HEADING . . . 1st row: With Green make 10 sc, ch 3 and 10 sc over each ch-15 across. Turn. **2nd row:** Sl st in next 5 sc, * ch 9, sc in next ch-3 loop, ch 9, skip 5 sc, tr in next sc, skip 4 sc on next loop, tr in next sc. Repeat from * across, ending with ch 5, skip 5 sc, tr in next sc. Ch 4, turn. **3rd row:** In next sp make (dc, ch 1) twice; ** dc in next sc, ch 1, * in next sp make (dc, ch 1) 4 times. Repeat from * once more. Repeat from ** across. Break off.

INSERTION . . . Work as for Edging No. EI-285 until the necessary number of flowers is completed. Attach Blue to center of last flower, * ch 15, sc in center of next flower. Repeat from * across. Break off.

Now with Green, work Heading as for Edging working on both sides of flowers. Make more flowers as necessary and tack them in place as illustrated with French knots.

EI-283 ᨑᨑᨑᨑ Rose
EDGING and INSERTION

MATERIALS:

J. & P. Coats Tatting-Crochet, Size 70, Rose (No. 46) and Bright Nile Green (No. 26-B) . . . Steel Crochet Hook No. 14.

EDGING—ROSE . . . Starting at center with Rose, ch 8. Join with sl st to form ring. **1st rnd:** 20 sc in ring. Sl st in first sc. **2nd rnd:** Ch 1, sc in same place as sl st, * ch 5, skip 3 sc, sc in next sc. Repeat from * around,

ending with sl st in first sc. **3rd rnd:** In each loop around make sc, half dc, 5 dc, half dc and sc. Sl st in next sc on previous rnd. **4th rnd:** * Ch 7, sc in next sc on 2nd rnd. Repeat from * around. **5th rnd:** In each loop around make sc, half dc, 7 dc, half dc and sc. Join and break off.

LEAF . . . Starting at tip with Green, ch 15. **1st row:** Sc in 2nd ch from hook, sc in each ch across to within last ch, 3 sc in last ch (this is tip of Leaf), sc in each ch along opposite side of starting chain, sc in same place as last sc. Mark last sc for base of Leaf. Hereafter pick up only the back loop of each sc. Do not turn but work sc in each sc to within 3 sc from center sc at tip of Leaf. Ch 1, turn. **2nd row:** Sc in each sc to within marked sc, 3 sc in marked sc, sc in each sc on other side to within 3 sc from center sc at tip of Leaf. Ch 1, turn. **3rd and 4th rows:** Sc in each sc to within center sc of 3-sc group, 3 sc in next sc, sc in each sc on other side to within last 3 sts. Ch 1, turn. **5th row:** Same as 3rd row, making sc, ch 7 and sc in center sc of sc-group at base of Leaf. **6th row:** Sc in back loop of each sc to within ch-7 loop, in loop make (3 sc, ch 5) 3 times and 3 sc; sc in back loop of each sc across to within last 3 sts. Break off. Make necessary number of roses and leaves, and tack together in alternate order, having a rose at both ends.

HEADING . . . 1st row: Attach Green to center st of 2nd free petal on Rose, ch 8, sc in center of next free petal, * ch 5, sc in next free picot on Leaf, ch 2, sc in next free picot, ch 5, tr in center sc on side of Leaf, ch 5, dc in center of next free petal on next Rose, ch 5, sc in center of next free

Continued on page 17.

EI-283

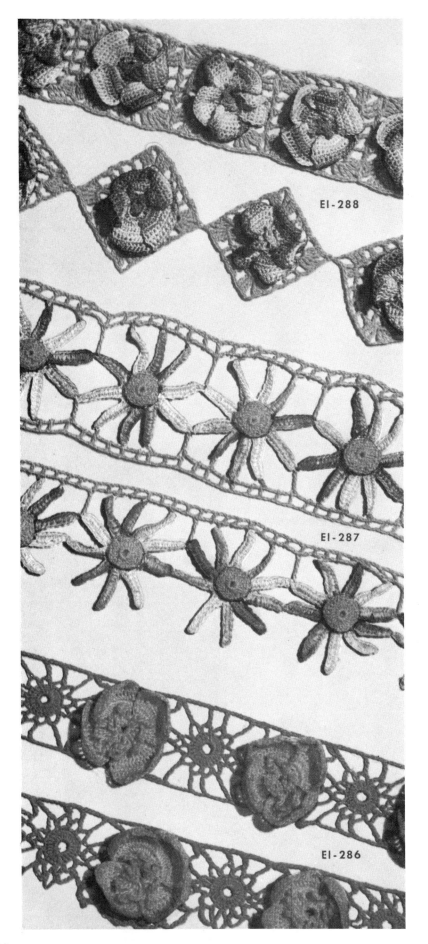

EI-288

EI-287

EI-286

More Flower Edgings

EI-288 Apple Blossom

← EDGING and INSERTION

MATERIALS:

J. & P. Coats Tatting-Crochet, Size 70, Shaded Pinks (No. 15), Shaded Yellows (No. 19) and Bright Nile Green (No. 26-B) . . . Steel Crochet Hook No. 14.

EDGING—FIRST MOTIF—Apple Blossom . . . Starting at center with Pinks, ch 8. Join with sl st to form ring. **1st rnd:** Ch 1, 25 sc in ring. Sl st in first sc. Now work petals individually as follows:

FIRST PETAL . . . 1st row: 2 sc in next 5 sc. Ch 1, turn. **2nd to 7th rows incl:** Sc in each sc across. Ch 1, turn. Do not turn at end of 7th row.

SECOND PETAL . . . Sl st in end sc of each row to base of petal. **Next row:** 2 sc in next 5 sc on center. Ch 1, turn and complete as for First Petal. Make 3 more petals same as Second Petal.

BASE . . . 1st rnd: Attach Green on 1st row (between petals), sc in same place, * ch 5, sc between next 2 petals on 1st row. Repeat from * around, ending with sl st in first sc. **2nd rnd:** Ch 3, 4 dc in each loop around. Sl st in first dc. **3rd rnd:** Ch 5, * dc in next dc, ch 2. Repeat from * around. Sl st in 3rd ch of ch-5. **4th rnd:** Ch 4, * in next sp make 2 tr, ch 3 and 2 tr; tr in next dc, (ch 2, dc in next dc) 3 times; ch 2, tr in next dc. Repeat from * around, ending with ch 2, sl st in top of ch-4. Break off.

CENTER . . . With Yellows make a chain 2 inches long. Make 5 loops of this chain to form stamens and sew in place at center of flower.

SECOND MOTIF . . . Work as for First Motif until 3rd rnd of base is completed. **4th rnd:** Ch 4, 2 tr in next sp, ch 1, sl st in any corner sp of First Motif, ch 1, 2 tr in same sp on Second Motif, tr in next dc, and complete as for First Motif (no more joinings).

Make necessary number of motifs, joining each to previous one as Second Motif was joined to First Motif (see illustration), having a free corner on each side of joining.

INSERTION—FIRST MOTIF . . . Work as for First Motif of Edging.

SECOND MOTIF . . . Work as for First Motif until 3rd rnd of Base is completed. **4th rnd:** Ch 4, in sp make 2 tr, ch 1, sl st in any corner sp on First Motif, ch 1, 2 tr in same sp on Second Motif, tr in next dc, ch 1, sl st in corresponding sp on First Motif, ch 1, dc in next dc on Second Motif, and complete as for First Motif, joining next three ch-2 sps and the following corner sp to corresponding sps of First Motif as before. Make necessary number of motifs, joining each to previous one as Second Motif was joined to First Motif.

EI-286 ___ Buttercup
EDGING and INSERTION

MATERIALS:

J. & P. Coats Tatting-Crochet, Size 70, Dk. Yellow (No. 43) and Hunter's Green (No. 48) . . . Steel Crochet Hook No. 14.

EDGING—BUTTERCUP MOTIF . . . Starting at center with Yellow, ch 6. Join with sl st to form ring.

FIRST PETAL . . . **1st row:** Sl st in ring, ch 3, 3 dc in ring. Ch 1, turn. **2nd row:** 2 sc in each dc, 2 sc in top of ch-3 (8 sc). Ch 3, turn. **3rd row:** Dc in first sc, 2 dc in each sc (16 dc, counting turning chain as 1 dc). Ch 1, turn. **4th row:** Sc in each st across (16 sc). Ch 3, turn. **5th row:** Skip first sc, dc in each sc across. Ch 1, turn. **6th row:** Sc in each st across. Ch 3, turn. **7th row:** Skip first sc, holding back on hook the last loop of each dc, make dc in next 3 sc, thread over and draw through all loops on hook (3 sts decreased), dc in each sc across, decreasing 3 sts at end of row as before. Ch 1, turn. **8th row:** (Insert hook in next st and draw loop through) 4 times; thread over and draw through all loops on hook (3 sts decreased), sc in each st across, decreasing 3 sts at end of row. Break off.

SECOND PETAL . . . Attach Yellow to ring, ch 3, 3 dc in ring and complete petal as before. Make 2 more petals in this manner.

BASE OF MOTIF . . . **1st rnd:** Attach Green in ring (between 2 petals), (ch 5, sc in ring between next 2 petals) 4 times. **2nd rnd:** Sl st in next ch-5 loop, ch 3, 5 dc in same loop, (6 dc in next loop) 3 times (24 dc, counting starting chain as 1 dc). **3rd rnd:** Sc in same place as sl st, * ch 5, skip next dc, sc in next dc. Repeat from * around, ending ch 5, sl st in first sc. **4th rnd:** Sl st to center of next loop, sc in same loop, * ch 5, sc in next loop. Repeat from * around. Join. **5th rnd:** Same as 4th rnd, making ch-6 (instead of ch-5). Break off.

CENTER . . . With double strand of Yellow, ch 1 loosely (ch 10 more sts in the usual manner, sc in the loose ch)

10 times. Break off. Sew center in place.

Make another Buttercup motif in this manner.

SMALL MOTIF . . . Starting at center with Green, ch 10. Join with sl st to form ring. **1st rnd:** Ch 3, 23 dc in ring. Sl st in top of ch-3. **2nd rnd:** Sc in same place as sl st, * ch 2, sl st in any loop on outer rnd of Buttercup Motif, ch 2, skip 1 dc on Small Motif, sc in next dc, ch 2, sl st in next loop on Buttercup Motif, ch 2, skip 1 dc on Small Motif, sc in next dc, (ch 5, skip 1 dc, sc in next dc) 4 times. Repeat from * once more, joining Small Motif to 2nd Buttercup Motif as before and ending with sl st in first sc. Break off.

Make necessary number of motifs, joining a Small Motif between 2 Buttercup Motifs as before, having 4 free loops on each side of joining on each motif.

HEADING . . . Attach Green to 3rd free loop preceding joining on end Buttercup Motif, sc in same place, * ch 3, sc in next loop, ch 5, d tr in next loop, d tr in next free loop on Small Motif, ch 5, tr in next loop, ch 3, tr in next loop, ch 5, d tr in next loop, d tr in next free loop on next motif, ch 5, sc in next loop. Repeat from * across. Break off.

SCALLOPED EDGE . . . Attach Green to 5th free loop on other side of end motif preceding joining, * ch 3, holding back on hook the last loop of each tr make 2 tr in next free loop, thread over and draw through all loops on hook (cluster made), ch 5, sc in 3rd ch from hook (picot made), ch 2, cluster in same loop, (in next loop make cluster, ch 2, picot, ch 2 and cluster) 3 times; ch 3, sc in next free loop on Small Motif, (ch 5, sc in next loop) 3 times. Repeat from * across. Break off. For Insertion, work Heading on both long sides

EI-287 ___ Aster
EDGING and INSERTION

MATERIALS:

J. & P. Coats Tatting-Crochet, Size 70, Shaded Dk. Blues (No. 14), Dk. Yellow (No. 43) and Hunter's Green (No. 48) . . . Steel Crochet Hook No. 14.

EDGING—FIRST ASTER . . . Starting at center with Blue, ch 8. Join with sl st to form ring. **1st rnd:**

Working over 4 strands make 20 sc in ring. Sl st in first sc. **2nd rnd:** * Make 10 sc over 4 strands (this starts petal); to complete petal—still working over 4 strands and the petal sts previously made make sc in 2nd sc from hook and in next 8 sc (one petal completed), sc in next 2 sc on ring. Repeat from * around (10 petals in all). Sl st in first sc. Break off.

CENTER . . . Starting at center with Yellow, ch 4. **1st rnd:** 19 dc in 4th ch from hook. Sl st in top of starting chain. **2nd rnd:** Sc in each st around. Sl st in first sc. **3rd rnd:** Ch 3, dc in each sc around. Sl st in top of starting chain. Stuff center and sew in place.

SECOND MOTIF . . . Work as for First Motif until first rnd is completed. **2nd rnd:** Make 10 sc over 4 strands, sl st in tip of any petal on First Motif. Working over 4 strands as before sc in 2nd sc from tip of petal and complete motif as before, joining tip of next petal to tip of corresponding petal of First Motif.

Make necessary number of motifs, joining each to previous one as Second Motif was joined to First Motif, having 3 petals free on each side of joinings.

HEADING . . . **1st rnd:** Attach Green to tip of 4th free petal on end motif preceding joining, ch 9, * dc in tip of next free petal, ch 5, sc in tip of next petal, ch 5, dc in tip of next petal, ch 5, tr in joining of petals, ch 5. Repeat from * across, ending with tr in tip of 4th free petal of last flower. Ch 5, turn. **2nd rnd:** * Dc in next sp, ch 2, skip same sp, dc in next st, ch 2. Repeat from * across. Break off.

INSERTION . . . Work as for Edging EI-287 making Heading on both long sides.

EI-283 Continued from page 15.

petal on Rose. Repeat from * across, ending with sc in center of next petal. Ch 5, turn. **2nd row:** * Dc in ch-5 sp, ch 2, dc in next dc, ch 2, dc in next ch-5 sp, ch 2, dc in next tr, ch 2, dc in next ch-5 sp, (ch 2, dc in next sc) twice; ch 2, dc in next ch-5 sp, ch 2, dc in next sc, ch 2. Repeat from * across, ending with dc in last ch-5 sp, ch 2, dc in 3rd st of turning ch-8. Break off.

INSERTION . . . Work as for Edging No. EI-283, making Heading on both long sides and being careful to have the same number of spaces.

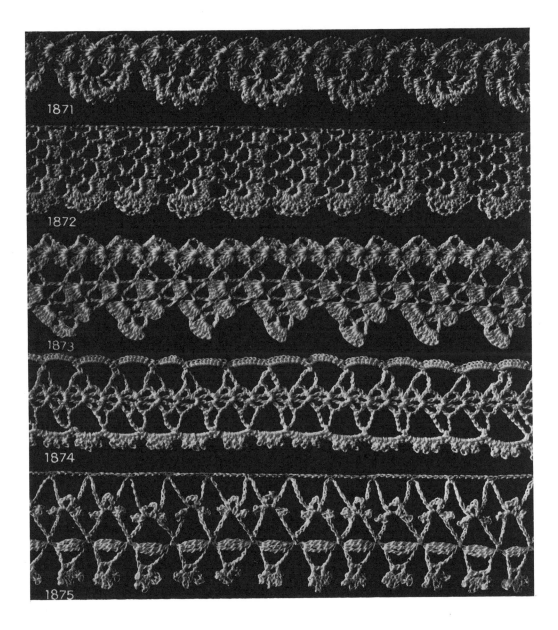

1871

1872

1873

1874

1875

Edgings for Gifts

Materials Suggested — AMERICAN THREAD COMPANY "STAR" or "GEM" MERCERIZED CROCHET COTTON
Sizes 30 to 50

No. 1871

Ch 5, 3 d c, ch 3, 3 d c in 4th st from hook, ch 3, turn.

2nd Row. 3 d c, ch 3, 3 d c in loop, ch 3, turn.

3rd Row. 3 d c, ch 3, 3 d c in loop, ch 5, turn.

4th Row. Shell in shell, ch 3, turn.

5th Row. Shell in shell, ch 2, 6 d c with ch 2 between in 5 ch loop, s c in 3 ch loop of previous row, turn, ch 3, 2 d c in first 2 ch loop, * sl st in next loop, ch 3, 2 d c in same loop, repeat from * 3 times, s c in next loop, ch 3, shell in shell, ch 3, turn.

Next Row. Shell in shell, ch 5, turn.

Next Row. Shell in shell, ch 3, turn, and repeat from 5th row for length desired.

No. 1872

Ch 22, s c in 10th st from hook, * ch 5, skip 3 chs, s c in next st, repeat from * twice, ch 5, turn.

2nd Row. S c in 1st loop, * ch 5, s c in next loop, repeat from * twice, ch 5, turn.

3rd Row. Repeat 2nd row.

4th Row. 3 d c in 1st loop, * ch 1, 3 d c in next loop, repeat from *, ch 1, 11 d c in next loop, sl st in loop of previous row, ch 3, turn.

5th Row. Skip 1 d c, s c in next d c, * ch 3, skip 1 d c, s c in next d c, repeat from * twice, * ch 5, skip 3 d c, s c in next 1 ch loop, repeat from * 3 times, ch 5, turn.

6th Row. S c in 1st loop, * ch 5, s c in next loop, repeat from * twice, ch 5, turn.

7th Row. S c in 1st loop, * ch 5, s c in next loop, repeat from * twice, ch 5, turn.

No 1872 *continued on page 27*

Instructions for 1873 to 1880 on pages 27 **and** *28*

1876

1877

1878

1879

1880

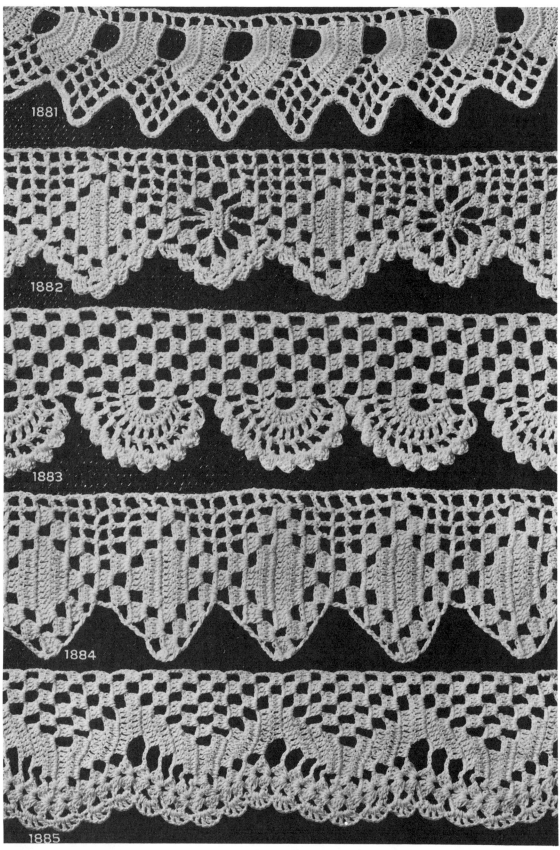

1881

1882

1883

1884

1885

A good idea is to make a roll of these edgings—keep them on hand for future use

Edgings for Now...

Instructions for Nos. 1881–1885 illustrated above on pages 28 to 30

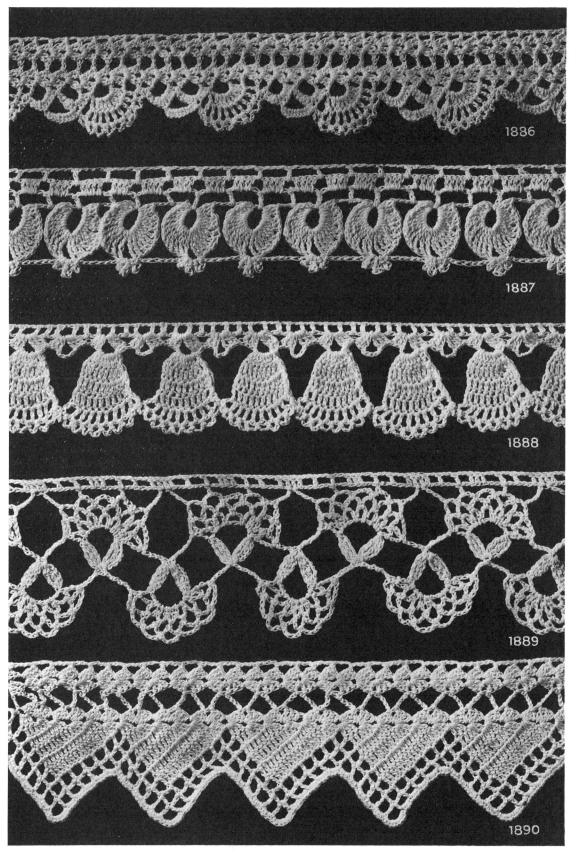

1886

1887

1888

1889

1890

Edgings for Later

Excellent as edgings for window shades, curtains, dressing table skirts, towels and sheet and pillow case sets

Instructions for Nos. 1886—1890 illustrated above on pages 30 and 31

Edgings for Guest Towels

J. & P. Coats Big Ball Best Six Cord Mercerized Crochet, Art. A.104, or Clark's Big Ball Mercerized Crochet, Art. B.34 . . . use Size 30 with Milwards Steel Crochet Hook No. 10, or use Size 50 with Milwards Steel Crochet Hook No. 12.

S-824 Starting at narrow end ch 20. **1st row:** Dc in 8th ch from hook, * ch 2, skip 2 ch, dc in next ch. Repeat from * across. Ch 5, turn (5 sps). **2nd and 3rd rows:** Skip first dc, (dc in next dc, ch 2) 4 times; skip 2 ch, dc in next ch. Ch 5, turn. **4th row:** Skip first dc, dc in next dc, ch 2, dc in next dc (2 sps). Ch 5, turn. **5th and 6th rows:** Skip first dc, dc in next dc, ch 2, skip 2 ch, dc in next ch. Ch 5, turn. At end of 6th row, ch 13, turn. **7th row:** Dc in 8th from hook, ch 2, skip 2 ch, dc in next ch, (ch 2, dc in next dc) twice; ch 2, skip 2 ch, dc in next ch. Ch 5, turn. Repeat 2nd to 7th rows incl until piece measures length desired, ending with 3rd row. Now work around outer edge as follows: Working across straight side and over 1 strand of "Speed-Cro-Sheen," make sc, ch 3 and sc in first sp, * sc at base of next dc, in next sp make sc, ch 3 and sc. Repeat from * across to next corner, in corner sp make (sc, ch 3) 3 times and sc; sc in next st, (in next sp make sc, ch 3 and sc; sc in next st) 3 times; in next sp make (sc, ch 3) 3 times and sc; sc in next st, in next sp make sc, ch 3 and sc; sc in next st, work next corner as before, in next sp make sc, ch 3 and sc; sc in next st, in next 2 sps make sc, ch 3 and sc; sc in next st. Complete rnd, omitting sc in st at inner edge of each corner. Join. Cut off "Speed-Cro-Sheen."

HEADING . . . Ch 5, * skip next ch 3 and 1 sc, dc in next sc, ch 2. Repeat from * across. Break off.

S-825 **FIRST FLOWER . . .** Starting at center, ch 6. Join with sl st to form ring. **1st rnd:** Working over a strand of "Speed-Cro-Sheen," make 12 sc in ring. Join. Drop "Speed-Cro-Sheen." **2nd rnd:** Sc in same place as sl st, * ch 15, sc in next 2 sc. Repeat from * around, ending with sc in last sc. Join. **3rd rnd:** Working over "Speed-Cro-Sheen," * in next loop make (2 sc, ch 3) 9 times and 2 sc; sl st between next 2 sc. Repeat from * around. Join and break off.

SECOND FLOWER . . . Work as for First Flower until 2 rnds have been completed. **3rd rnd:** Working over "Speed-

Cro-Sheen," in next loop make (2 sc, ch 3) 4 times and 2 sc; ch 1, sl st in center ch-3 loop of any petal on First Flower, ch 1, in same loop on Second Flower make (2 sc, ch 3) 4 times and 2 sc; sl st between next 2 sc. Complete rnd (no more joinings).

Make desired number of flowers, joining as Second Flower was joined to First Flower and leaving 2 petals free between joinings on each flower.

HEADING . . . 1st row: Attach thread to center ch-3 loop on 2nd petal preceding joining on First Flower, sc in same place, * ch 5, skip 1 ch-3 loop, holding back on hook the last loop of each dc, make dc in next loop and in corresponding loop on next petal, thread over and draw through all loops on hook (joint dc made); ch 5, skip 1 loop, sc in next loop, ch 7, skip 1 loop; holding back on hook the last loop of each st make tr in next loop, skip 3 loops on next petal, d tr in next loop, then make d tr and tr in corresponding loops of next flower, thread over and draw through all loops on hook (joint cluster made); ch 7, skip 1 loop, sc in next loop. Repeat from * across, ending with joint dc, ch 5, skip 1 loop, sc in next loop. Ch 6, turn. **2nd row:** * Dc in next sp, ch 3, dc in next joint dc, ch 3, dc in next sp, ch 3, dc in next sc, ch 3, dc in next sp, ch 3, dc in next cluster, ch 3, dc in next sp, ch 3, dc in next sc, ch 3. Repeat from * across. Ch 6, turn. **3rd row:** Skip first dc, * dc in next dc, ch 3. Repeat from * across. Break off.

S-826 Starting at narrow end, ch 11. **1st row:** Dc in 4th ch from hook, dc in next ch, ch 5, skip 5 ch, in next ch make dc, ch 3 and dc. Ch 1, turn. **2nd row:** Insert hook in first loop, draw loop through, thread over and draw through both loops on hook, then draw loop on hook out to measure ½ inch, (retaining all loops on hook, insert hook in same sp, draw loop through, thread over and draw through loop on hook and up to height of last loop) 9 times; insert hook in same sp, draw thread through, thread over and complete a sl st, ch 7, sc in next sp, ch 3, dc in next

dc, ch 1, skip next dc, dc in top of turning chain. Ch 3, turn. **3rd row:** Skip first dc, dc in next sp, dc in next dc, ch 5, skip next sc and 3 ch, dc in next ch, (ch 2, sc in next loop) 10 times. Ch 5, turn. **4th row:** Skip first sc, (dc in next sc, ch 2) 9 times; dc in next dc, ch 3, sc in next sp, ch 3, dc in next dc, ch 1, skip next dc, dc in top of turning chain. Ch 3, turn. **5th row:** Skip first dc, dc in next sp, dc in next dc, ch 5, in next dc make dc, ch 3 and dc. Ch 1, turn. Repeat 2nd to 5th rows incl until piece measures length desired, ending with 4th row. Break off.

SCALLOPED EDGE . . . 1st row: Attach thread to first free sp on 4th row of edging, sc in same place, * (ch 3, sc in next sp) 5 times; ch 1, sc in first sp on next scallop. Repeat from * across. Break off.

S-827 **LEAF . . .** Starting at center, ch 26. **1st row:** Sc in 2nd ch from hook, ch 4, skip 3 ch, dc in next ch, ch 4, skip 3 ch, tr in next ch, ch 4, skip 3 ch, d tr in next ch, ch 4, skip 3 ch, tr in next ch, ch 4; skip 3 ch, dc in next ch, ch 4, skip 3 ch, sc in next ch; now work along opposite side of starting chain to correspond, ending with sl st in first sc. Break off.

Make necessary number of leaves for length desired.

To Join Leaves: With right side of leaf facing, attach thread to sl st, now, working over "Speed-Cro-Sheen" (in next sp make 3 sc, ch 3—picot made —and 3 sc) 6 times; ch 3, (in next sp make 3 sc, ch 3 and 3 sc) 6 times. Join with a sl st to first sc. Now working over the "Speed-Cro-Sheen" only make (3 sc, ch 3) 7 times and 3 sc. Work around second leaf as before to within last 4 sps, make 3 sc in next sp, ch 1, sl st in the 4th picot on first leaf, ch 1, 3 sc in same sp where last 3 sc were made on second leaf, make 3 sc in next sp, ch 1, sl st in corresponding picot on preceding leaf, ch 1, 3 sc in same sp where last 3 sc were made on second leaf. Complete as for first leaf. Continue in this manner until all leaves have been joined.

S-824

S-825

S-826

S-827

Edgings for Café Curtains

J. & P. Coats Big Ball Best Six Cord Mercerized Crochet, Art. A.104, or Clark's Big Ball Mercerized Crochet, Art. B.34 ... use Size 20 with Milwards Steel Crochet Hook No. 9, or use Size 30 with Milwards Steel Crochet Hook No. 10.

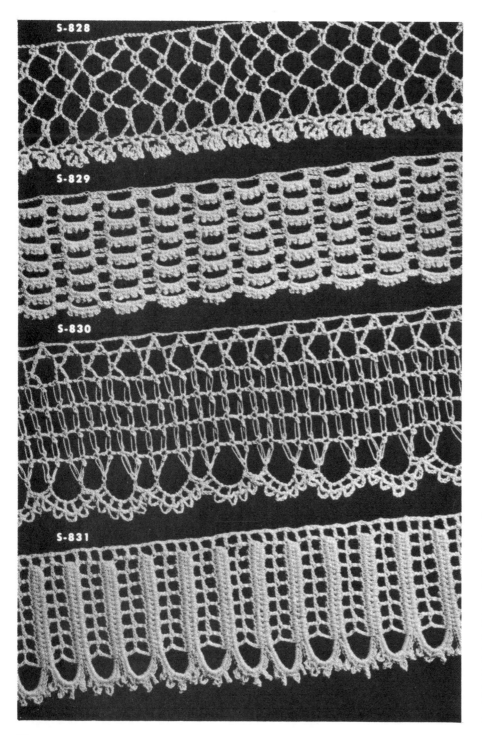

S-828 Starting at narrow edge, ch 23. **1st row:** Sc in 11th ch from hook, (ch 3, skip next ch, sc in next ch, ch 7, skip next 2 ch, sc in next ch) twice; ch 3, skip next ch, sc in last ch. Ch 5, turn. **2nd row:** In first ch-3 loop make (dc, ch 3) 5 times; (in next ch-7 loop make sc, ch 3, sc, and ch 7) twice; in last loop make sc, ch 3 and sc. Ch 10, turn. **3rd row:** (In next ch-7 loop make sc, ch 3, sc, and ch 7) twice; skip next ch-3 loop and next sp, in next sp make sc, ch 3 and sc. Ch 5, turn. Repeat 2nd and 3rd rows alternately until piece measures length desired, ending with 2nd row. Break off.

S-829 Starting at long side, make a chain slightly longer than length desired. **1st row:** Sc in 2nd ch from hook, * ch 7, skip 4 ch, sc in next ch, ch 3, skip 3 ch, sc in next ch. Repeat from * until row measures length desired, ending with a ch-7 loop. Cut off remaining chain. Ch 1, turn. **2nd row:** * In next ch-7 loop make (2 sc, ch 3) 5 times and 2 sc; ch 3. Repeat from * across. Ch 1, turn. **3rd row:** Sc in first ch-3 loop, * ch 7, skip 3 loops, sc in next loop, ch 3, skip next sp, sc in next loop. Repeat from * across. Ch 1, turn. **4th to 13th rows incl:** Repeat 2nd and 3rd rows alternately 5 times more. **14th row:** Repeat 2nd row. Break off.

S-830 Starting at narrow edge, ch 19. **1st row:** Draw loop on hook out to measure ¼ inch, thread over and draw loop through, insert hook between single and double loops and draw loop through, thread over and draw through 2 loops on hook (knot st made); make another knot st, dc in first ch, (make 1 knot st, skip next 3 ch, dc in next ch) 3 times; ch 3, skip next 2 ch, sc in next ch, ch 3, skip next 2 ch, dc in next ch (a lacet made). Ch 8, turn. **2nd row:** Skip first dc and next sc, dc in next dc (1 bar made over a lacet), (make 1 knot st, dc in next dc) 3 times; make 2 knot sts. Turn. **3rd row:** Dc in first dc, (make 1 knot st, dc in next dc) 3 times; ch 3, sc in next sp, ch 3, dc in 3rd ch of ch-8 (another lacet). Ch 8, turn. Repeat 2nd and 3rd rows alternately until piece measures length desired, ending with 3rd row and having a number of rows divisible by 4, plus 1; ch 8.

Continued on next page

S-830

HEADING . . . 1st row: Working across long side, holding back on hook the last loop of each dc, make dc at base of last dc made and dc in top of next dc, thread over and draw through all loops on hook (joint dc made), * ch 5, make joint dc by making dc at base of same dc and in top of next dc. Repeat from * across, ending with ch 5, dc at base of last dc. Break off.

SCALLOPED EDGE . . . 1st row: With wrong side of Heading facing, attach thread to knot at center of first knot st loop, sc in same place, * ch 10, sc in knot at center of next knot st loop, ch 5, sc in next knot st loop. Repeat from * across. Ch 8, turn. **2nd row:** Dc in 6th ch from hook, dc in ch-10 loop, in same loop make (ch 5, dc in last dc made, dc in ch-10 loop) 4 times; * sc in ch-5 loop, dc in next loop, in same loop make (ch 5, dc in last dc made, dc in same loop) 5 times. Repeat from * across. Break off.

S-831

Starting at narrow edge, ch 23. **1st row:** Working over a strand of "Speed-Cro-Sheen," make sc in 2nd ch from hook and in each ch across. Ch 5, turn. Drop "Speed-Cro-Sheen." **2nd row:** Skip first 3 sc, dc in next sc, * ch 2, skip next 2 sc, dc in next sc. Repeat from * across. Ch 5, turn. **3rd row:** Skip first dc, * dc in next dc, ch 2. Repeat from * across, ending with ch 2, dc in 3rd ch of turning chain. Ch 1, turn. **4th row:** Place "Speed-Cro-Sheen" at top of last row—allowing for a 3/8 inch loop at beginning of row—and, working over it, make sc in first dc, * 2 sc in next sp, sc in next dc. Repeat from * across, ending with 2 sc in last sp, sc in 3rd ch of turning chain. Ch 1, turn. **5th row:** Continuing to work over "Speed-Cro-Sheen," make sc in each sc across. Ch 5, turn. Drop "Speed-Cro-Sheen." Repeat 2nd to 5th rows incl for length desired, ending with 4th row. Break off.

HEADING . . . Attach thread to ch at base of first sc made, ch 5, * dc in next dc, ch 2, dc at base of next sc, ch 2, dc in next sc on next row, ch 2. Repeat from * across. Break off.

SCALLOPED EDGE . . . Attach thread to first sc made on last row on opposite side, * make 5 sc in next "Speed-Cro-Sheen" loop, ch 5, in same loop make (3 sc, ch 5) 3 times and 5 sc; sl st in side of next sc row. Repeat from * across. Break off.

⟦ S-675 ⟧
Illustrated on Page 7

COATS & CLARK'S O.N.T. TATTING-CRO-CHET, Art. C.21, Size 70: 1 ball of No. 12-D Shaded Black and White.

Milwards Steel Crochet Hook No. 14.

A rolled edge handkerchief, 13½ inches square.

1st rnd: Attach thread to edge of handkerchief 3/16 inch preceding any corner, ch 5, in corner make dc, ch 5 and dc; * ch 2, skip 3/16 inch on edge, make a dc. Repeat from * around, making dc, ch 5 and dc in each corner and having a number of sps divisible by 3, including one corner sp on each side. Join to 3rd ch of ch-5. **2nd rnd:** Sl st in next sp, sc in same sp, * ch 7, skip next sp, sc in next sp, ch 3, sc in next sp. Repeat from * around. Join. **3rd rnd:** Sl st in next loop, ch 3, 5 dc in same loop, * (ch 3, sc in last dc made) 3 times (triple picot made); 5 dc in same loop, sc in next loop, 5 dc in next loop. Repeat from * around. Join and break off.

⟦ S-676 ⟧
Illustrated on Page 7

COATS & CLARK'S O.N.T. TATTING-CRO-CHET, Art. C.21, Size 70: 3 balls of No. 1 White.

Milwards Steel Crochet Hook No. 14.

A rolled edge handkerchief, 14½ inches square.

1st rnd: Attach thread to any corner, 5 sc in same corner, sc closely around (18 sc to 1 inch), making 5 sc in each corner. Join with sl st. **2nd rnd:** Sl st to center sc of 5-sc group, ch 4, holding back on hook the last loop of each tr make 2 tr in same sc, thread over and draw through all loops on hook (cluster made); ch 5, make 3-tr cluster in same sc, (ch 5, skip next 2 sc, 3-tr cluster in next sc) twice; skip next 4 sc, cluster in next sc (last 2 clusters made make a joint cluster), * (ch 5, skip next 2 sc, cluster in next sc) 3 times; skip next 4 sc, cluster in next sc (another joint cluster made). Repeat from * across side, ending with a joint cluster ¼ inch from next corner, ch 5, skip next 2 sc, cluster in next sc, ch 5, in center sc of 5-sc group at corner make cluster, ch 5 and cluster; (ch 5, skip next 2 sc, cluster in next sc) twice; skip next 4 sc, cluster in next sc. Complete other sides and corners the same way. Join to tip of first cluster. **3rd rnd:** Sl st in next sp, ch 4, in same sp make 2-tr cluster, ch 3 and 3-tr cluster; ch 5, * in next sp make 3-tr cluster, ch 3 and 3 tr cluster; ch 7, sc in next sp, ch 7, sc in tip of next joint cluster, ch 7, sc in next sp, ch 7. Repeat from * across side, ending with sc in tip of joint cluster preceding next corner, ch 7, sc in next sp, ch 7, (in next sp make cluster, ch 3 and cluster, ch 5) twice; in next sp make cluster, ch 3 and cluster; ch 7, sc in next sp, ch 7, sc in tip of next joint cluster. Complete other sides and corners the same way. Join. **4th rnd:** Sl st in next ch-3 sp between clusters, ch 6, sl st in 3rd ch from hook (picot made), make 2 more picots, dc in same sp, ch 5, sc in next sp, * ch 5, in next sp between clusters make dc, 3 picots and dc; (ch 5, sc in each of next 2 ch-7 loops) twice. Repeat from * across side, ending with dc, 3 picots and dc in first ch-3 sp between clusters on next corner group of clusters, (ch 5, sc in next sp, ch 5 in next sp between clusters make dc, 3 picots and dc) twice; (ch 5, sc in each of next 2 ch-7 loops) twice. Complete other sides and corners the same way. Join to 3rd ch of ch-6. Break off.

No. 1813

Ch 12, d c in 8 st from hook, ch 3, d c in end, ch 3, turn.

2nd Row. D c in 1st loop, * ch 3, thread over, insert in same loop, pull through, thread over, work off 2 loops, thread over, insert in same loop, pull through, thread over and work off 2 loops at a time, repeat from * twice, ch 3, 4 cluster sts in next loop with ch 3 between, ch 5, turn.

3rd Row. S c in 3 ch loop, * ch 5, s c in next loop, repeat from * 3 times, ch 3, turn, and repeat 2nd and 3rd rows for any length desired, break thread.

Fasten thread at top of edging, * ch 6, skip next loop, s c in 1st loop of next scallop, repeat from * and continue across row.

No. 1814

Ch 5, 3 d c, ch 2, 3 d c in 5th st from hook, ch 4, turn.

2nd Row. 3 d c, ch 2, 3 d c in 2 ch loop, skip 2 d c, tr c in next d c, ch 4, turn.

3rd Row. 3 d c, ch 2, 3 d c in 2 ch loop, tr c in 4 ch loop of previous row, ch 4, turn, and repeat 3rd row for length desired.

On one end of insertion work scallop as follows—
9 tr c with ch 1 between in 1st loop, * ch 2, skip 1 loop, s c in next loop, ch 2, skip 1 loop, 9 tr c with ch 1 between in next loop and repeat from * across row.

Next Row. Ch 3, s c between next 2 tr c, * ch 3, s c between next 2 tr c, repeat from * across shell, ch 3, sl st in s c of previous row, ch 3, s c between next 2 tr c and repeat from beginning across row.

No. 1815

Ch 17, d c in 8th st from hook, * ch 2, skip 2 sts, d c in next st, repeat from * twice, ch 5, turn.

2nd Row. D c in next d c, 5 d c in next mesh, slip loop off hook, insert into 1st of the 6 d c and draw loop through (this is termed a popcorn st) ch 2, popcorn st in next mesh, ch 2, d c in next d c, ch 2, d c in 3rd st of ch, ch 5, turn.

3rd Row. 2 open meshes, ch 4, sl st in top of last d c for picot, 2 open meshes, ch 5, turn.

4th Row. 1 open mesh, ch 5, skip 2 open meshes, 1 open mesh, ch 5, turn.

5th Row. 1 open mesh, ch 3, s c in center st of ch 5, ch 3, 1 open mesh, ch 5, turn.

6th Row. 1 open mesh, ch 2, skip 2 chs, s c in next ch, d c in s c, 1 s c in next ch, ch 2, 1 open mesh, ch 5, turn.

7th Row. 1 open mesh, ch 3, s c in d c, ch 3, 1 open mesh, ch 5, turn.

8th Row. 1 open mesh, ch 7, sl loop off hook, insert hook into 3rd and last st and draw loop through, this forms a picot turned down, ch 2, 1 open mesh, ch 5, turn.

9th Row. 4 open meshes, ch 5, turn and repeat from the 2nd row for length desired.

Working along long edge, ch 1, * 2 s c in next mesh, s c in next st, picot, 2 s c in next mesh, ch 1, skip next st and mesh, in next st, work (d c, picot, ch 1) 3 times; repeat from * across edge. Fasten off.

No. 1816

Ch for desired length, d c in 8th st from hook, * ch 2, skip 2 chs, d c in next ch, repeat from * across row, turn.

2nd Row. Sl st into mesh, ch 4, d c in same mesh, * ch 6, sl st in 4th st from hook for picot, ch 2, skip 1 mesh, 2 d c with ch 1 between in next mesh, repeat from * across row.

3rd and 4th Rows. Same as 2nd row working 1 d c, ch 2, 1 d c in each shell.

5th Row. 4 d c, picot, 4 d c in 1st shell, ch 2, d c in next shell, ch 5, sl st in 4th st from hook for picot, ch 1, d c in same shell, ch 2, repeat from beginning across row.

No. 1817

Ch for desired length, d c in 8th st from hook, * ch 2, skip 2 sts, d c in next st, repeat from * across row, ch 1, turn.

2nd Row. 3 s c in each mesh, ch 5, turn.

3rd Row. Skip 2 s c, d c in next s c, * ch 2, skip 2 s c, d c in next s c, repeat from * across row, ch 7, turn.

4th Row. Skip 1 mesh, 2 s c in next mesh, * ch 7, skip 1 mesh, 2 s c in next mesh, repeat from * ch 3, turn.

5th Row. 5 d c over loop, ch 7, turn, sl st in 1st d c made, ch 1, turn, 9 s c over loop, ch 5, s c in each s c, ch 3 and repeat from beginning.

No. 1830

Ch 17, 1 d c in 4th st from hook, 1 d c in each of the next 2 chs, ch 2, skip 2 chs, d c in next ch, ch 5, sl st in 4th st from hook for picot, ch 1, skip 2 chs, d c in next ch, ch 2, skip 2 chs, 1 d c in each of the next 3 chs, ch 3, turn.

2nd Row. 1 d c in each of the next 2 d c, ch 8, 1 d c in each of the 3 end d c, ch 3, turn.

3rd Row. 1 d c in each of the next 2 d c, ch 2, skip 2 chs, 1 d c in each of the next 4 chs, ch 2, skip 2 chs, 1 d c in each of the 3 end d c, ch 3, turn.

4th Row. Same as 2nd row.

5th Row. 1 d c in each of the next 2 d c, ch 2, skip 2 chs, 1 d c in next ch, ch 5, sl st in 4th st from hook for picot, ch 1, skip 2 chs, d c in next ch, ch 2, 1 d c in each of the next 3 d c, ch 3, turn and repeat from 2nd row for length desired.

No. 1831

Ch 20, d c in 8th st from hook, * ch 2, skip 2 chs, d c in next ch, repeat from * 3 times, ch 5, turn.

2nd Row. 1 o m, 1 s m, 1 o m, 1 s m, 1 o m, ch 5, turn.

3rd Row. 5 open meshes.

4th Row. 1 o m, ch 8, skip 2 d c, d c in next ch, 1 o m, ch 5, turn.

5th Row. D c in d c, * ch 2, skip 2 chs, d c in next ch, repeat from *, ch 2, d c in d c, 1 o m, ch 5, turn.

6th Row. Same as 4th row.

7th Row. Same as 5th row. Repeat from 2nd row for length desired.

Scallop. 4 d c with ch 1 between in mesh, * s c in next mesh, 4 d c with ch 1 between in next mesh, repeat from * across row, break thread and work other side to correspond.

No. 1832

Make a ch a little longer than desired and work a row of d c on ch, turn.

2nd Row. * ch 5, thread over twice, skip 2 d c, insert in next d c and work off 2 loops twice, thread over twice, insert in same space and work off 2 loops twice, thread over twice, insert in same space and work off all loops 2 at a time, ch 5, sl st through top of cluster st for picot, ch 5, skip 2 d c, s c in next d c, repeat from * across row, break thread. Make a second piece joining to 1st piece at picots as follows: ch 2, sl st into corresponding picot of 1st section, ch 2, sl st through top of cluster st being made, repeat from beginning.

No. 1833

Ch 36, d c in 8th st from hook, 1 d c in each of the next 2 chs, ch 9, skip 8 chs, d c in next ch, ch 2, skip 2 chs, d c in next ch, ch 9, skip 8 chs, 1 d c in each of the next 3 chs, ch 2, skip 2 chs, d c in end ch, ch 5, turn.

2nd Row. 1 d c in each of the next 3 d c, ch 8, d c in

d c, ch 2, d c in next d c, ch 8, 1 d c in each of the next 3 d c, ch 2, skip 2 chs, d c in next ch, ch 5, turn.

3rd Row. 1 d c in each of the next 3 d c, * ch 4, skip the row below, s c in center st of loop of previous row, ch 4, d c in d c, * ch 2, d c in next d c, repeat between *s, 1 d c in each of the next 2 d c, ch 2, d c in 3rd st of ch 5, ch 5, turn.

4th Row. 1 d c in each of the next 3 d c, ch 9, d c in next d c, ch 2, d c in next d c, ch 9, 1 d c in each of the next 3 d c, ch 2, d c in 3rd st of ch, ch 5, turn and repeat from 2nd row for length desired.

Scallop. 2 s c in 1st mesh, 3 s c in next mesh, picot and repeat from beginning across row.

Work other edge to correspond.

No. 1872 *continued from page 18*

8th Row. 3 d c in 1st loop, * ch 1, 3 d c in next loop, repeat from *, ch 1, 11 d c in next loop, s c in next loop of previous row, ch 3, turn.

9th Row. Skip 1 d c, s c in next d c, * ch 3, skip 1 d c, s c in next d c, repeat from * twice, * ch 5, skip 3 d c, s c in next 1 ch loop, repeat from * twice, ch 5, s c in end loop, ch 5, turn and repeat from 6th row for length desired.

Designs shown on page 18

No. 1873

Ch 11, 2 d c, ch 2, 3 d c in 5th st from hook, ch 3, skip 2 chs, d c in next ch, ch 3, d c in same st, skip 2 chs, d c in next ch, ch 3, d c in same space, ch 3, turn.

2nd Row. 5 d c in 1st loop, ch 1, 6 d c in next loop, ch 3, skip next loop, s c in next d c, ch 1, 3 d c, ch 2, 3 d c in next loop, ch 4, turn.

3rd Row. Shell in shell, ch 3, skip 3 d c, d c in next d c, ch 3, d c in same space, skip 5 d c, d c in ch 1 between groups of d c, ch 3, d c in same space, skip 3 d c, d c in next d c, ch 3, d c in same space, ch 3, turn.

4th Row. 5 d c in 1st loop, * ch 1, 6 d c in next loop, repeat from *, ch 3, s c in next d c, ch 1, 3 d c, ch 2, 3 d c in next 2 ch loop, ch 4, turn.

5th Row. Shell in shell, ch 3, skip 3 d c, d c in next d c, ch 3, d c in same space, skip 5 d c, d c, ch 3, d c in 1 ch loop, ch 3, turn and repeat from 2nd row for length desired.

No. 1874

Ch 10, d c in 6th st from hook, * ch 2, d c in same space, repeat from * twice, ch 2, skip 3 sts, s c in next st, ch 7, turn, 4 d c with ch 2 between in 3rd 2 ch loop, * ch 7, turn, 4 d c with ch 2 between in center loop, repeat from * for desired length, ch 9 and across one side work * 1 s c in loop, ch 7 and repeat from * across row, ch 1, turn and work 9 s c over each mesh. Break thread.

Join thread to loop on other side of edging and work 1 s c in each loop with ch 7 between each s c.

Next Row. 3 s c, picot, 2 s c, picot, 2 s c, picot, 2 s c in each loop, break thread.

No. 1875

Ch 10, s c in 5th st from hook for a p (ch 5, p), twice, skip these 3 picots, d c in next ch st, ch 3, a 3 tr c cluster st in 1st st of work, * ch 11, p (ch 5, p), twice, skip these 3 picots, d c in next ch st, ch 3, skip 3 chs, a 3 tr c cluster st in next ch st. Repeat from * for required length.

2nd Row (Ch 8, p, ch 6, p, ch 4, s c between next 2 clusters) repeat from beginning to end of row. Fasten off.

3rd Row. Join between 1st 2 ps, ch 5, s c in same space (ch 11, s c between next 2 ps, ch 5, s c in same space), repeat to end of row.

4th Row. Ch 12, turn, s c in last 11 ch loop (ch 6, s c in next loop), repeat to end of row, Ch 7, tr c between 2 end picots. Fasten off.

Designs shown on page 19

Materials Suggested — AMERICAN THREAD COMPANY "STAR" or "GEM" MERCERIZED CROCHET COTTON Sizes 10 to 70

No. 1876

Ch 18, d c in 6th st from hook, ch 3, d c in same space, * ch 2, skip 3 sts, 2 d c with ch 3 between in next st, repeat from * ch 4, turn.

2nd Row. 3 d c with ch 3 between in first loop, skip the 2 ch, 4 d c with ch 3 between in next 3 ch loop, skip next 2 ch loop, 2 d c with ch 3 between in next loop, ch 2, s c in same space, ch 2, 2 d c with ch 3 between in same loop, ch 2, d c in 3rd st of ch, ch 5, turn.

3rd Row. Skip the 2 chs, 2 d c with ch 3 between in next loop, ch 2, skip the next d c, s c and d c, 2 d c with ch 3 between in next loop, * ch 2, 2 d c with ch 3 between in center loop of 4 d c shell, repeat from *, ch 4, turn.

4th Row. 3 d c with ch 3 between in 1st loop, * 4 d c with ch 3 between in next 3 ch loop, repeat from *, 2 d c with ch 3 between in next 3 ch loop, ch 2, s c in same loop, ch 2, 2 d c with ch 3 between in same loop, ch 2, d c in 3rd st of ch 5, ch 5, turn.

5th Row. Same as 3rd row having 5—2 d c shells in row, ch 4, turn.

6th Row. Same as 4th row having 5 shells across row, ch 5, turn.

7th Row. Same as 5th row having 6—2 d c shells in row, ch 4, turn.

8th Row. Same as 6th row having 6 shells across row, ch 5, turn.

9th Row. 2 d c with ch 3 between in 3 ch loop, ch 2, skip the next d c, s c, d c, 2 d c with ch 3 between in next loop, * ch 2, 2 d c with ch 3 between in center loop of next 4 d c, repeat from *, ch 4, turn and repeat from 4th row for length desired.

No. 1877

Ch 19, d c in 12th st from hook, ch 5, skip 4 sts, 1 d c in each of 3 end chs, ch 3, turn.

2nd Row. 1 d c in next 2 d c, 3 d c in loop, ch 5, 4 d c with ch 3 between in end loop, ch 5, turn.

3rd Row. Skip 1st loop, 3 d c with ch 3 between in next loop, ch 5, skip next loop, 3 d c in next loop, 1 d c in each of the next 6 d c, ch 3, turn.

4th Row. 1 d c in each of the next 8 d c, 3 d c in 5 ch loop, ch 5, skip next loop, 4 d c with ch 3 between in next loop, ch 5, turn.

5th Row. Skip 1st loop, 3 d c with ch 3 between in next loop, ch 5, skip next loop, 3 d c in next loop, 1 d c in each of the next 12 d c, ch 3, turn.

6th Row. 1 d c in each of the next 14 d c, 3 d c in 5 ch loop, ch 5, skip next loop, 4 d c with ch 3 between in next loop, ch 5, turn.

7th Row. 3 d c with ch 3 between in center loop of shell, ch 5, 2 d c in 5 ch loop, 1 d c in d c, ch 5, skip 4 d c, 2 d c with ch 3 between in next d c, ch 5, skip 5 d c, 2 d c with ch 3 between in next d c, ch 5, skip 5 d c, 2 d c with ch 3 between in next d c, ch 4, turn.

8th Row. 3 d c with ch 3 between in 1st loop, *, ch 2, skip 5 ch loop, 4 d c with ch 3 between in next loop, repeat from * ch 5, 1 d c in each of the next 3 d c, 3 d c in 5 ch loop, ch 5, 4 d c with ch 3 between in center loop of shell, ch 5, turn.

9th Row. 3 d c with ch 3 between in center loop of shell, ch 5, 3 d c in 5 ch loop, 1 d c in each of the next 6 d c, ch 5, shell in center loop of shell * ch 2, shell in center loop of next shell, repeat from * ch 4, turn.

10th Row. 3 d c with ch 3 between in center loop of 1st shell * ch 2, shell in center loop of next shell, repeat from *, ch 5, 1 d c in each of the next 9 d c, ch 5, 3 d c in ch, ch 5, shell in center loop of shell, ch 5, turn.

11th Row. 3 d c with ch 3 between in center loop of shell, ch 5, 3 d c in 5 ch loop, 1 d c in each of the next 12 d c, ch 5, shell in shell, * ch 2, shell in shell, repeat from *, ch 4, turn.

12th Row. Shell in shell * ch 2, shell in next shell, repeat from *, ch 5, 1 d c in each of the next 15 d c, 3 d c in ch, ch 5, shell in shell, ch 5, turn.

13th Row. Shell in shell, ch 5, 2 d c in 5 ch loop, 1 d c in d c, ch 5, skip 4 d c, 2 d c with ch 3 between in next d c, * ch 5, skip 5 d c, 2 d c with ch 3 between in next d c, repeat from * once, * ch 2, shell in shell, repeat from * twice, ch 4, turn.

14th Row. Shell in shell, * ch 2, shell in next shell, repeat from * 4 times, ch 5, 1 d c in each of the next 3 d c, 3 d c in ch, ch 5, shell in shell, ch 5, turn.

15th Row. Shell in shell, ch 5, 3 d c in 5 ch loop, 1 d c in each of the next 6 d c, ch 5, shell in shell, * ch 2, shell in next shell, repeat from * 4 times, ch 4, turn.

16th Row. Shell in shell, * ch 2, shell in next shell, repeat from * 4 times, ch 5, 1 d c in each of the next 9 d c, 3 d c in 5 ch loop, ch 5, shell in shell, ch 5, turn.

17th Row. Shell in shell, ch 5, 3 d c in 5 ch loop, 1 d c in each of the next 12 d c, ch 5, shell in shell, * ch 2, shell in next shell, repeat from * 4 times, ch 4, turn.

18th Row. Shell in shell, * ch 2, shell in next shell, repeat from * 4 times, ch 5, 1 d c in each of the next 15 d c, 3 d c in 5 ch loop, ch 5, shell in shell, ch 5, turn.

Repeat from 13th row for desired length.

No. 1878

Ch 10, join to form a ring, ch 3, 8 d c in ring, ch 3, s c in ring, ch 5, turn.

2nd Row. S c in 3 ch loop, ch 4, skip 1 d c, s c in next d c, ch 5, skip 5 d c, s c in end d c, ch 3, turn.

3rd Row. 7 d c in 5 ch loop, ch 4, s c in next loop, ch 4, s c in next loop, ch 5, turn.

4th Row. ** S c in first loop, ch 4, s c in next loop, ch 4, skip 1 d c, s c in next d c, ch 5, skip 5 d c, s c in end d c, ch 3, turn.

5th Row. 7 d c in 5 ch loop, * ch 4, s c in next loop, repeat from * twice, ch 5, turn.

6th Row. S c in 1st loop, * ch 4, s c in next loop, repeat from *, ch 4, skip 1 d c, s c in next d c, ch 4, skip 2 d c, s c in next d c, ch 4, s c in end d c, ch 4, s c between 2nd and 3rd shell, ch 4, s c in 3 ch loop, ch 6 turn, sl st in 4th st from hook for picot, ch 2, s c in 1st loop, * ch 6, slip st in 4th st from hook for picot, ch 2, s c in next loop, repeat from * 5 times, ch 4, s c in end loop, ch 5, turn.

7th Row. S c in 1st loop, ch 5, s c in next loop, ch 3, turn.

8th Row. 7 d c in 5 ch loop, ch 4, s c in end loop, ch 5, turn.

Next Row. S c in 1st loop, ch 4, skip 1 d c, s c in next s c, ch 5, s c in end d c, ch 2, sl st in 1st picot, turn, ch 6, sl st in 4th st from hook for picot, ch 2, s c in 5 ch loop, ch 3, 7 d c in same loop, * ch 4, s c in next loop,

repeat from * ch 5, turn and repeat from the 4th row for length desired.

For a straight edge ch 7 to turn.

No. 1879

Ch for desired length and work a row of 2 ch meshes.

2nd Row. 5 d c in each of the 1st two meshes * ch 2, skip 1 mesh, d c in next mesh, ch 2, d c in same mesh, ch 2, skip 1 mesh, 5 d c in each of the next 2 meshes and repeat from * across row.

3rd Row. * 8 d c over the 10 d c, ch 2, d c in center loop, ch 2, d c in same loop, ch 2 and repeat from * across row.

4th Row. * 6 d c over the 8 d c of previous row, ch 3, d c in center loop, ch 2, d c in same loop, ch 3 and repeat from * across row.

5th Row. 4 d c over the 6 d c of previous row, ch 3, d c in center loop, * ch 2, d c in same loop, repeat from *, ch 3 and repeat from beginning across row.

6th Row. * 2 d c over the 4 d c of previous row, ch 3, skip 1st loop, 2 d c with 2 ch between in next loop, ch 2, 2 d c with 2 ch between in next loop, ch 3 and repeat from * across row.

7th Row. Ch 3, skip the 3 ch loop, 2 d c with ch 2 between in next loop, * ch 2, 2 d c with ch 2 between in next loop, repeat from * ch 3, s c between 2 d c of previous row and repeat from beginning across row.

8th Row. Work a row of s c and picot.

No. 1880

Ch 9, 2 d c in 8th st from hook, 2 d c in next st, ch 3, turn.

2nd Row. D c in same st, 2 d c in each of the next 3 d c, ch 2, tr c in 3rd st of ch, ch 5, turn.

3rd Row. 2 d c in 1st d c, 2 d c in next d c, * ch 2, skip 2 d c, d c in next d c, repeat from * ch 5, turn.

4th Row. D c in d c, ch 2, 2 d c in each of the next 4 d c, ch 2, tr c in 3rd st of ch, ch 5, turn and repeat 3rd and 4th rows for length desired.

Work a row of s c across bottom of scallop.

Designs shown on page 20

Materials Suggested — AMERICAN THREAD COMPANY "STAR" or "GEM" MERCERIZED CROCHET COTTON Sizes 10 to 50

No. 1881

Ch 10, d c in 1st ch, ch 3, turn.

2nd Row. 14 d c in loop, ch 3, turn.

3rd Row. 1 d c in each of the next 14 d c, ch 3, turn.

4th Row. 1 d c in each of the next 14 d c, ch 10, turn.

5th Row. Skip 5 d c, d c in next d c, * ch 2, skip 1 d c, d c in next d c, repeat from * 3 times, ch 5, turn.

6th Row. D c in d c, * ch 2, d c in next d c, repeat from * twice, 13 d c in loop, d c in 4th st of ch, ch 3, turn.

7th Row. 1 d c in each of the next 14 d c, * ch 2, d c in next d c, repeat from * twice, ch 2, d c in 3rd st of ch, ch 5, turn.

8th Row. D c in d c, * ch 2, d c in next d c, repeat from * twice, 1 d c in each of the next 14 d c, ch 10, turn and repeat from 5th row for length desired.

Work a row of 2 ch meshes across top and a row of s c around lower edge of scallops.

No. 1882

Ch 25, d c in 8th st from hook, 1 d c in each of the next

2 sts, * ch 2, skip 2 sts, d c in next st, repeat from * 4 times, ch 5, turn.

2nd Row. D c in d c, * ch 2, d c in next d c, repeat from *, ch 2, skip next d c, 3 d c in loop, ch 2, skip 3 d c, 3 d c in next loop, 1 tr c in same loop, ch 5, turn.

3rd Row. 3 d c in tr c loop, * ch 2, 3 d c in next loop, repeat from * ch 2, skip next d c, d c in next d c, ch 2, d c in next d c, ch 2, d c in 3rd st of ch, ch 5, turn.

4th Row. D c in d c, ch 2, skip next d c, 3 d c in next loop, ch 2, 3 d c in next loop, 1 d c in each of the next 3 d c, 3 d c in next loop, ch 2, 3 d c in ch 5 loop, tr c in same space, ch 5, turn.

5th Row. 3 d c in tr c loop of previous row, ch 2, 3 d c in next loop, 1 d c in each of the next 9 d c, 3 d c in next loop, ch 2, 3 d c in next loop, ch 2, d c in 3rd st of ch, ch 5, turn.

6th Row. D c in d c, ch 2, skip 2 d c, 3 d c in next loop, ch 2, skip 3 d c, 1 d c in each of the next 9 d c, ch 2, skip 3 d c, 3 d c in next loop, skip 2 d c, 1 tr c in next d c, ch 5, turn.

7th Row. 3 d c in loop, ch 2, skip 3 d c, 1 d c in each of the next 3 d c, ch 2, skip 3 d c, 3 d c in next loop, ch 2, skip 2 d c, d c in next d c, ch 2, d c in next d c, ch 2, d c in 3rd st of ch, ch 5, turn.

8th Row. D c in d c, * ch 2, d c in next d c, repeat from *, ch 2, 3 d c in next loop, ch 2, 3 d c in next loop, skip 2 d c, tr c in next d c, ch 5, turn.

9th Row. 3 d c in next loop, ch 2, skip 2 d c, d c in next d c, * ch 2, d c in next d c, repeat from * twice, ch 2, d c in 3rd st of ch, ch 5, turn.

10th Row. D c in d c, * ch 2, d c in next d c, repeat from *, ch 2, skip next d c, 3 d c in next loop, ch 2, 3 d c in end loop, tr c in same loop, ch 5, turn.

11th Row. 3 d c in tr c loop, ch 5, tr c in next loop, ch 5, skip 3 d c, 3 d c in next loop, ch 2, skip next d c, d c in next d c, ch 2, d c in next d c, ch 2, d c in 3rd st of ch, ch 5, turn.

12th Row. D c in d c, ch 2, skip next d c, 3 d c in next loop, ch 5, skip 3 d c, 1 s c in next loop, 1 s c in tr c, 1 s c in next loop, ch 5, skip 3 d c, 3 d c in end loop, tr c in same loop, ch 5, turn.

13th Row. 3 d c in tr c loop, ch 5, skip 3 d c, 1 s c in next loop, 1 s c in each of the next 3 s c, 1 s c in next loop, ch 5, skip 3 d c, 3 d c in next loop, ch 2, d c in 3rd st of ch, ch 5, turn.

14th Row. D c in d c, ch 2, skip 2 d c, 3 d c in next loop, ch 5, 1 s c in each of the 3 center s c, ch 5, 3 d c in next loop, skip 2 d c, tr c in next d c, ch 5, turn.

15th Row. 3 d c in loop, ch 2, tr c in center s c, ch 2, 3 d c in next loop, ch 2, skip 2 d c, d c in next d c, ch 2, d c in next d c, ch 2, d c in 3rd st of ch, ch 5, turn.

16th Row. D c in d c, * ch 2, d c in next d c, repeat from *, ch 2, skip 2 d c, 3 d c in next loop, ch 2, 3 d c in next loop, skip 2 d c, tr c in next d c, ch 5, turn.

17th Row. Skip 3 d c, 3 d c in 2 ch loop, ch 2, skip 2 d c, d c in next d c, * ch 2, d c in next d c, repeat from * twice, ch 2, d c in 3rd st of ch, ch 5, turn and repeat from 2nd row for length desired.

Scallop. * ch 3, 2 d c in same space, sl st in next loop and repeat from * across lace skipping the loop between each scallop.

No. 1883

Ch 23, d c in 9th st from hook, 1 d c in each of the next 2 chs, * ch 3, skip 3 ch, 1 d c in each of the next 3 chs, repeat from * ch 5, turn.

2nd Row. Skip 2 d c, 3 d c in next loop, * ch 3, 3 d c in next loop, repeat from *, ch 8, turn.

3rd Row. D c in 1st d c, * ch 3, 3 d c in next loop, repeat from * twice, ch 5, turn.

4th Row. 3 d c in next loop, * ch 3, 3 d c in next loop, repeat from *, 11 d c in next loop, sl st in 5 ch loop, ch 4, turn.

5th Row. 1 d c in each d c with ch 1 between (12 d c counting ch 4 as a d c), * ch 3, 3 d c in next loop, repeat from * twice, ch 5, turn.

6th Row. 3 d c in 1st loop, * ch 3, 3 d c in next loop, repeat from *, ch 2, 1 d c with ch 2 between in each of the next 11 loops, s c in corner st of previous row, ch 3, turn.

7th Row. 2 d c in next loop, sl st in next loop, * ch 3, 2 d c in same loop, sl st in next loop, repeat from *, 8 times, ch 5, 3 d c in next loop, * ch 3, 3 d c in next loop, repeat from * ch 5, turn.

8th Row. 3 d c in next loop, * ch 3, 3 d c in next loop, repeat from * ch 5, turn.

9th Row. Repeat 8th row.

10th Row. 3 d c in next loop, * ch 3, 3 d c in next loop, repeat from * ch 8, turn and repeat from 3rd row for length desired.

No. 1884

Ch 23, d c in 8th st from hook, * ch 2, skip 2 sts, d c in next st, repeat from * twice, ch 2, skip 2 sts, 1 d c in each of the next 4 sts, ch 1, tr c in same space, ch 6, turn.

2nd Row. 4 d c in next loop, ch 2, skip 4 d c, 4 d c in next loop, ch 2, skip next d c, d c in next d c, * ch 2, d c in next d c, repeat from *, ch 2, d c in 5th st of ch, ch 5, turn.

3rd Row. D c in d c, ch 2, d c in next d c, ch 2, skip next d c, 4 d c in next loop, * ch 2, skip 4 d c, 4 d c in next loop, repeat from *, ch 2, tr c in same loop, ch 6, turn.

4th Row. 4 d c in 1st loop, ch 2, skip 4 d c, 3 d c in next loop, 1 d c in each of the next 4 d c, 3 d c in next loop, ch 2, skip 4 d c, 4 d c in next loop, ch 2, skip next d c, d c in next d c, ch 2, d c in 3rd st of ch, ch 5, turn.

5th Row. Skip loop and 1 d c, 4 d c in next loop, ch 2, skip 4 d c, 3 d c in next loop, 1 d c in each of the next 10 d c, 3 d c in next loop, ch 2, skip 4 d c, 4 d c in next loop, ch 1, tr c in same space, ch 4, turn.

6th Row. Skip 4 d c, 4 d c in next loop, ch 2, skip 3 d c, 1 d c in each of the next 10 d c, ch 2, skip 3 d c, 4 d c in next loop, ch 2, skip 3 d c, d c in next d c, ch 2, d c in 3rd st of ch, ch 5, turn.

7th Row. D c in d c, ch 2, d c in next d c, ch 2, skip 3 d c, 4 d c in next loop, ch 2, skip 3 d c, 1 d c in each of the next 4 d c, ch 2, skip 3 d c, 4 d c in next loop, skip 3 d c, tr c in next d c, ch 4, turn.

8th Row. Skip 4 d c, 4 d c in next loop, ch 2, skip 4 d c, 4 d c in next loop, ch 2, skip 3 d c, d c in next d c, * ch 2, d c in next d c, repeat from *, ch 2, d c in 3rd st of ch, ch 5, turn.

9th Row. D c in d c, * ch 2, d c in next d c, repeat from * twice, ch 2, skip 3 d c, 4 d c in next loop, ch 1, skip 3 d c, tr c in next d c, ch 6, turn.

10th Row. 4 d c in 1 ch loop, ch 2, skip 4 d c, 4 d c in next loop, ch 2, skip 1 d c, d c in next d c, * ch 2, d c in next d c, repeat from *, ch 2, d c in 3rd st of ch, ch 5, turn and repeat from 3rd row for length desired.

No. 1885

Ch 26, 3 d c, ch 2, 3 d c in 8th st from hook, ch 3, skip 3 sts, 1 d c in each of the next 9 sts, ch 3, skip 3 sts, 1 d c in each of the next 3 sts, ch 5, turn.

Continued on next page

2nd Row. Skip 3 d c, 3 d c in 3 ch loop, ch 3, skip 3 d c, 1 d c in each of the next 6 d c, 3 d c in loop, ch 3, skip next 3 d c, 3 d c, ch 2, 3 d c in next 2 ch loop, tr c in 2nd st of ch, ch 4, turn.

3rd Row. Skip 3 d c, 3 d c, ch 2, 3 d c in 2 ch loop, ch 3, 3 d c in next loop, 1 d c in each of the next 6 d c, ch 3, skip 3 d c, 3 d c in next loop, ch 3, 3 d c in end loop, ch 5, turn.

4th Row. 3 d c in loop, ch 3, 3 d c in next loop, ch 3, skip 3 d c, 1 d c in each of the next 6 d c, 3 d c in loop, ch 3, skip 3 d c, 3 d c, ch 2, 3 d c in next 2 ch loop, tr c in top of 1st d c of previous row, ch 4, turn.

5th Row. 3 d c, ch 2, 3 d c in 2 ch loop, ch 3, 3 d c in next loop, 1 d c in each of the next 6 d c, ch 3, skip 3 d c, 3 d c in next loop, * ch 3, 3 d c in next loop, repeat from *, ch 5, turn.

6th Row. 3 d c in loop, * ch 3, 3 d c in next loop, repeat from *, ch 3, skip 3 d c, 1 d c in each of the next 6 d c, 3 d c in loop, ch 3, shell in shell, 1 tr c in top of 1st d c of previous row, ch 4, turn.

7th Row. Shell in shell, ch 3, skip the loop and 3 d c, 1 d c in each of the next 6 d c, 3 d c in loop, * ch 3, 3 d c in next loop, repeat from * twice, ch 5, turn.

8th Row. 3 d c in loop, * ch 3, 3 d c in next loop, repeat from *, 1 d c in each of the next 6 d c, ch 3, skip 3 d c and loop, shell in shell, tr c in top of 1st d c of previous row, ch 4, turn.

9th Row. Shell in shell, ch 3, skip loop and 3 d c, 1 d c in each of the next 6 d c, 3 d c in next loop, * ch 3, 3 d c in next loop, repeat from *, ch 5, turn.

10th Row. 3 d c in loop, ch 3, 3 d c in next loop, 1 d c in each of the next 6 d c, ch 3, shell in shell, tr c in top of 1st d c of previous row, ch 4, turn.

11th Row. Shell in shell, ch 3, skip loop and 3 d c, 1 d c in each of the next 6 d c, 3 d c in loop, ch 3, 3 d c in next loop, ch 5, turn.

12th Row. 3 d c in loop, ch 3, skip 3 d c, 1 d c in each of the next 6 d c, 3 d c in loop, ch 3, shell in shell, tr c in top of 1st d c of previous row, ch 4, turn and repeat from 3rd row for length desired.

Border. 4 d c with ch 1 between in 1st loop, sl st in next loop, * 4 d c with ch 1 between in next loop, sl st in next loop and repeat from * across row.

Designs shown on page 21

Materials Suggested — AMERICAN THREAD COMPANY "STAR" or "GEM" MERCERIZED CROCHET COTTON Sizes 10 to 70

No. 1886

Ch 7, 1 d c, ch 1, 2 d c in 4th st from hook, ch 1, skip 2 chs, 2 d c, ch 1, 2 d c in next st, ch 3, turn.

2nd Row. 2 d c, ch 1, 2 d c in next loop, ch 1, skip the next 2 d c, ch 1, and 2 d c and work 2 d c, ch 1, 2 d c in next loop, ch 3, turn.

3rd Row. Shell in shell, ch 1, shell in next shell, ch 5, sl st in ch 3 of previous row, ch 1, turn.

4th Row. 9 s d c over 5 ch loop, ch 1, shell in shell, ch 1, shell in next shell, d c in 3 ch loop of previous row, ch 3, turn.

5th Row. Shell in shell, ch 1, shell in next shell, ch 5, sl st in ch 1 of previous row, ch 1, turn.

6th Row. 5 s d c over loop just made, ch 5, turn, sl st in 5th s d c of first scallop, ch 1, turn, 9 s d c over loop just made, 4 s d c over other half of 2nd scallop * ch 1, shell in shell, repeat from *, d c in 3 ch loop of previous row, ch 3, turn.

7th Row. Shell in shell, ch 1, shell in next shell, ch 5, sl st in 1 ch loop of previous row, ch 3, turn.

8th Row. 8 d c in loop just made * ch 1, shell in shell, repeat from *, d c in 3 ch loop of previous row, ch 3, turn.

9th Row. Shell in shell, ch 1, shell in next shell, ch 1, skip 2 d c, 1 d c with ch 1 between in each of the next 9 d c, ch 1, sl st in 5th s d c of bottom scallop, ch 3, turn.

10th Row. S c in ch 1 between 2 d c * ch 3, s c between next 2 d c and repeat from * 7 times, ch 2, shell in shell, ch 1, shell in next shell, d c in 3 ch loop of previous row, ch 3, turn.

11th Row. Shell in shell, ch 1, shell in next shell, ch 5, sl st in next loop of previous row, ch 1 turn, and repeat from 4th row for length desired.

No. 1887

1st Row. Ch 10, join to form a ring. * Work 3 d c, 3 tr c, 6 d tr c, ch 1, 6 d tr c, 3 tr c, 3 d c into ring, ch 16, sl st in 10th st from hook and repeat from * for desired length.

2nd Row. Ch 6, d c in center of ch, * ch 4, d c in base of ring, ch 4, d c in center of ch, repeat from * to end of row.

3rd Row. 4 d c over ch, * ch 1, 4 d c over next ch, repeat from * to end of row.

4th Row. Ch 5, * d c between groups of d c, ch 3, repeat from * to end of row.

Picot Edge. Join thread to center of ring, * ch 4, sl st in same st, ch 5, sl st in same st, ch 4, sl st in same st, ch 7, sl st in center of next ring and repeat from * to end of row.

No. 1888

Ch for desired length, d c in 5th st from hook, * ch 1, skip 1 ch, d c in next ch, repeat from * across row, turn.

2nd Row. Ch 3, skip 1 mesh, 3 d c, ch 5, 3 d c in next mesh, ch 1, turn, sl st into 5 ch loop, ch 3, 7 d c in same loop, ch 3, turn, 1 d c in same space, 1 d c in each of the next 6 d c, 2 d c in next d c, * ch 3, turn, 1 d c in each d c, repeat from *, ch 4, turn, 1 d c with ch 1 between in each d c, ch 4, turn, sl st between next 2 d c, * ch 4, sl st between next 2 d c, repeat from * 7 times, sl st down side of bell and 3 d c, * skip 2 meshes, 3 d c, ch 5, 3 d c in next mesh, repeat from *, ch 1, turn, sl st into loop, ch 3, 7 d c in same loop, ch 3, turn, 1 d c in same space, 1 d c in each of the next 6 d c, 2 d c in next d c, * ch 3, turn, 1 d c in each d c, repeat from * ch 4, 1 d c in each d c with ch 1 between, join to 1st bell with a sl st, ch 4, turn and finish same as 1st bell.

No. 1889

Ch 6, work a 2 tr c cluster st in 1st st, * ch 8, 3 tr c cluster st in same st. Ch 5, turn, s c over 8 ch, (ch 4, s c over 8 ch), 5 times, ch 4, s c in next cluster st, ch 6, turn, s c in last 4 ch loop, (ch 4, s c in next loop), 6 times. ** Ch 4, turn, s c in last 4 ch loop, (ch 4, s c in next loop), 6 times. Ch 11, a 2 tr c cluster st in 6th st from hook. Repeat from * to **, 1 tr c in st at base of 2 cluster sts of previous Fan, repeat from ** until enough Fans are completed for required length.

Heading Rows. Ch 8, turn, 1 tr c in 2nd 4 ch loop (ch 6, d c in next loop, ch 7, d c in 2nd loop, ch 6, tr c in next loop, tr c in 2nd loop on next Fan), repeat to end of row. Fasten off.

2nd Row. Join to 1st tr c, ch 3, * d c in next ch st, ch 2, skip 2 sts of ch, d c in next st, ch 2, d c in next d c, ch 2, skip 2 ch sts, d c in next 3 sts, ch 2, d c in next d c (ch 2, skip 2 sts of ch, 1 d c in next st), twice, d c in next 2 tr c. Repeat from * to end of row.

Ch 21, d c in 5th st from hook, 1 d c in each of the next 3 chs, ch 2, 1 d c in each of the next 3 chs, ch 4, skip 3 sts, 3 d c, ch 2, 3 d c in next st, * ch 2, skip 2 sts, d c in next st, repeat from *, ch 5, turn.

2nd Row. D c in d c, ch 2, 1 d c in each of the next 3 d c, 3 d c, ch 2, 3 d c in 2 ch loop, skip 2 d c, s c in next d c, ch 4, skip loop and 3 d c, 3 d c, ch 2, 3 d c in next loop, d c in ch 4 loop of previous row, ch 4, turn.

3rd Row. 3 d c, ch 2, 3 d c in 2 ch loop, skip 2 d c, s c in next d c, ch 4, skip loop and 3 d c, 3 d c, ch 2, 3 d c in next 2 ch loop, 1 d c in each of the next 6 d c, ch 2, d c in d c, ch 2, d c in 3rd st of ch, ch 5, turn.

4th Row. D c in d c, ch 2, 1 d c in each of the next 9 d c, 3 d c, ch 2, 3 d c in next 2 ch loop, skip 2 d c, s c in next d c, ch 4, shell in shell, tr c in 4 ch loop of previous row, ch 4, turn.

5th Row. Shell in shell, skip 2 d c, s c in next d c, ch 4, shell in shell, 1 d c in each of the next 12 d c, ch 2, d c

in next d c, ch 2, d c in 3rd st of ch, ch 5, turn.

6th Row. D c in d c, ch 2, 1 d c in each of the next 15 d c, 3 d c, ch 2, 3 d c, in 2 ch loop, skip 2 d c, s c in next d c, ch 4, shell in shell, tr c in 4 ch loop of previous row, ch 4, turn.

7th Row. Shell in shell, skip 2 d c, s c in next d c, ch 4, shell in shell, * ch 2, skip 2 d c, d c in next d c, repeat from * 5 times, ch 2, d c in next d c, ch 2, d c in 3rd st of ch, ch 5, turn.

8th Row. D c in d c * ch 2, d c in next d c, repeat from * 6 times, 1 d c in each of the next 2 d c, 3 d c, ch 2, 3 d c in 2 ch loop, skip 2 d c, s c in next d c, ch 4, shell in shell, tr c in 4 ch loop of previous row, ch 4, turn.

9th Row. Shell in shell, skip 2 d c, s c in next d c, ch 4, shell in shell, 1 d c in each of the next 6 d c, ch 2, d c in next d c, ch 2, d c in next d c, ch 5, turn and repeat from 4th row for length desired.

Work 3 s c in each loop and 7 s c in each point of scallop.

6601
6602
6603
6604
6605
6606

Lovely, frosty, crocheted edging — Make your home,
your children's clothing, your lingerie sparkle with lace
that will serve as heirloom treasures.

Edgings of Many Uses

The edgings shown on the opposite page can be made with the following AMERICAN THREAD COMPANY products.

For	Materials Required	Needle
Handkerchiefs—	STAR Tatting Cotton Article 25	13
Lingerie or Sheets and Cases	STAR Crochet Cotton Article 20 or 30, Size 30 or	11
	GEM Crochet Cotton Article 35, Size 30	11
Towels or Tablecloths or Doilies	SILLATEEN SANSIL Article 101 or	10
	STAR Pearl Cotton Article 90 or	7
	DELUXE Crochet and Knitting Cotton Article 346 or	7
	PURITAN Mercerized Cotton Article 40	7

White or colors desired

Crocheted Edging No. 6601

Steel Crochet Hook No. 13.
Ch for desired length, d c in 8th st from hook, * ch 3, sl st in top of d c just made for picot, ch 3, skip 3 sts of ch, 1 d c in each of the next 5 sts of ch, ch 7, turn, sl st in top of 1st d c of 5 d c group, ch 1, turn, 5 s c, ch 4, 5 s c over loop just made, sl st in top of last d c, ch 3, skip 3 sts of ch, d c in next st, repeat from * across row, break thread.

Crocheted Edging No. 6602

Ch for desired length, d c in 8th st from hook, * ch 2, skip 2 sts of ch, d c in next st, repeat from * across row, ch 3, turn.
2nd Row—* 2 d c in next mesh, d c in next d c, ch 2, d c in next d c, ch 2, d c in next d c, repeat from * across row having a multiple of 3 meshes ending with the single d c.
3rd Row—* Ch 7, sl st in 4th st from hook for picot, ch 3, skip 1 d c, 1 s c in each of the next 2 d c, ch 7, sl st in 4th st from hook for picot, ch 3, s c in the single d c, repeat from * across row, break thread.

Crocheted Edging No. 6603

Ch for desired length, d c in 8th st from hook, * ch 2, skip 2 sts of ch, d c in next st, repeat from * across row, ch 5, turn.
2nd Row—* D c in next d c, d c in next d c, ch 5, repeat from * across row ending row with d c in 3rd st of ch, ch 7, turn.
3rd Row—S c in next d c, * ch 7, s c in 1st d c of next 2 d c group, repeat from * across row, ch 1, turn.
4th Row—3 s c, ch 4 (picot loop), 3 s c, ch 4, 3 s c over 1st loop, 3 s c, ch 4, 2 s c over next loop, ch 8, turn, skip 2 picot loops, sl st in center st between picots of 1st loop, ch 1, turn and work 3 s c, ch 4, 2 s c, ch 4, 2 s c, ch 4, 3 s c over loop just made, sl st in last s c of previous loop, 1 s c, ch 4, 3 s c over remainder of same loop, repeat from beginning across row, break thread.

Crocheted Edging No. 6604

Ch for desired length, d c in 8th st from hook, * ch 2, skip 2 sts of ch, d c in next st, repeat from * across row, ch 1, turn.
2nd Row—* 3 s c in next mesh, 2 s c in next mesh, repeat from * across row, ch 6, turn.
3rd Row—Skip 3 s c, s c in next s c, * ch 6, skip 3 s c, s c in next s c, repeat from * across row, ch 6, turn.
4th Row—S c in next loop, * ch 6, s c in next loop, repeat from * across row, ch 6, turn.

5th Row—2 cluster sts with ch 3 between in next loop (cluster st: thread over hook, insert in space, pull through and work off 2 loops, thread over hook, insert in same space, pull through and work off 2 loops, thread over and work off all loops at one time), ch 3, s c in next loop, ch 3, repeat from beginning across row in same manner ending row with 2 cluster sts with ch 3 between in last loop, turn.
6th Row—Sl st to loop between the cluster sts, ch 7, sl st in 3rd st from hook for picot, ch 1, d c in same space, * ch 4, sl st in 3rd st from hook for picot, ch 1, d c in same space, ch 4, sl st in 3rd st from hook for picot, ch 1, d c in same space, ch 3, s c in next s c, ch 3, sl st in last s c for picot, ch 3, d c between next 2 cluster sts, ch 4, sl st in 3rd st from hook for picot, ch 1, d c in same space, repeat from * across row, break thread.

Crocheted Edging No. 6605

Crochet a ch for desired length, s c in 8th st from hook, * ch 5, skip 3 sts of ch, s c in next st, repeat from * across row, ch 5, turn.
2nd Row—S c in next loop, * ch 5, s c in next loop, repeat from * across row, ch 5, turn.
3rd Row—S c in first loop, * ch 3, 3 cluster sts with ch 2 between each cluster in next loop (cluster st: thread over hook twice, insert in loop, pull through and work off 2 loops twice, thread over hook twice, insert in same space, pull through and work off 2 loops twice, thread over and work off all loops at one time), ch 3, s c in next loop, ch 5, s c in next loop, repeat from * across row ending row with 3 cluster sts with ch 2 between each cluster st in next loop, ch 3, turn.
4th Row—* S c in next loop between cluster sts, ch 3, s c between next 2 cluster sts, ch 3, s c in next loop, ch 3, d c in next loop, ch 2, d c in same loop, ch 3, s c in next loop, ch 3, repeat from * across row ending row with s c in next loop between cluster sts, ch 3, s c between next 2 cluster sts, ch 3, s c in next loop, ch 3, s c in next loop, ch 7, turn.
5th Row—Skip first loop, s c in next loop, ch 3, s c in next loop, ch 3, s c in next loop, ch 3, skip next loop, 1 d c, ch 2, 1 d c, ch 2, 1 d c in next loop, ch 3, skip next loop, s c in next loop, repeat from * across row, ending row with ch 3, s c in next loop, ch 3, s c in next loop, ch 5, turn.
6th Row—S c in first loop, * ch 3, skip next loop, d c in next loop, ch 2, d c in same loop, ch 2, d c in next loop, ch 2, d c in same loop, ch 3, skip next loop, s c in next loop, ch 3, s c in next loop, repeat from * across row ending row with ch 3, s c in last loop, ch 7, turn.
7th Row—Skip next loop, ** s c in next loop, ch 5, sl st in 4th st from hook for picot, ch 1, s c in same space, ch 3, skip 1 loop, s c in next loop, ch 5, sl st in 4th st from hook for picot, ch 1, s c in same space, * s c in next loop, ch 1, picot, ch 1, s c in same space, repeat from * once, ch 3, skip 1 loop, repeat from ** across row, break thread.

Crocheted Edging No. 6606

Ch 20, d c in 4th st from hook, 1 d c in next st of ch, ch 3, skip 2 sts of ch, sl st in next st, ch 3, skip 2 sts of ch, 1 d c in each of the next 3 sts, ch 6, skip 6 sts of ch, d c in end st, * ch 3, d c in same st, repeat from * twice, ch 1, turn.
2nd Row—S c in last d c made, * 5 d c in next loop, s c in next d c (petal), repeat from * twice, ch 5, 1 d c in each of the next 3 d c, ch 5, 1 d c in each of the next 2 d c, d c in 3rd st of ch, ch 3, turn.
3rd Row—1 d c in each of the next 2 d c, * ch 3, sl st in center st of ch 5, ch 3, 1 d c in each of the next 3 d c, ch 6, d c in center d c of center petal, * ch 3, d c in same st, repeat from * twice, ch 1, turn.
Repeat 2nd and 3rd rows for length desired.

Filigree Edgings

No. 8-56 Make a chain slightly longer than length desired. **1st row:** In 6th ch from hook make 2 dc, ch 3 and 2 dc; * ch 2, skip 3 ch, sc in next ch, ch 2, skip 3 ch, in next ch make 2 dc, ch 3 and 2 dc. Repeat from * across. Ch 3, turn. **2nd row:** Skip first dc, dc in next dc, * ch 2, 2 dc in next sp, (ch 2. dc in next 2 dc) twice. Repeat from * across, ending with dc in last 2 dc. Ch 3, turn. **3rd row:** Skip first dc, dc in next dc, * ch 2, holding back on hook the last loop of each dc make 2 dc in first dc, thread over and draw through all loops on hook (cluster made), ch 5, cluster in next dc, ch 2, (make one cluster over the next 2 dc) twice. Repeat from * across. Break off.

No. 8-57 Make a chain slightly longer than length desired. **1st row:** Dc in 5th ch from hook, * ch 1, skip 1 ch, dc in next ch. Repeat from * across. Ch 1, turn. **2nd row:** * Sc in next sp, ch 5, holding back on hook the last loop of each tr make 2 tr in next sp, thread over and draw through all loops on hook (cluster made), ch 6, sc in 6th ch from hook, (ch 5, sc in same place as last sc was made) twice; ch 5, sc in next sp, ch 3. Repeat from * across. Break off.

No. 8-58 Make a chain slightly longer than length desired. **1st row:** In 6th ch from hook make 2 dc, ch 2 and 2 dc (shell made), * ch 5, skip 4 ch, sc in next ch, ch 3, skip 1 ch, sc in next ch, ch 5, skip 4 ch, in next ch make 2 dc, ch 2 and 2 dc (another shell made). Repeat from * across. Ch 5, turn. **2nd row:** * Shell in sp of next shell (shell made over shell), ch 5, sc in ch-5 sp, ch 3, sc in next sp, ch 3, sc in next ch-5 sp, ch 5. Repeat from * across. Ch 5, turn. **3rd row:** * Shell over shell, ch 6, sc in next ch-3 loop, ch 3, sc in next loop, ch 6. Repeat from * across. Ch 5, turn. **4th row:** * In sp of next shell make (sc, ch 5) 3 times and sc; ch 7, sc in next ch-3 loop, ch 7. Repeat from * across. Break off.

No. 8-59 Starting at narrow end, ch 6. **1st row:** Holding back on hook the last loop of each dc make 2 dc in 6th ch from hook, thread over and draw through all loops on hook (cluster

made), ch 3, cluster in same place as last cluster was made. Ch 5, turn. **2nd row:** In ch-3 sp make cluster, ch 3 and cluster. Ch 5, turn. Repeat the 2nd row for length desired.

Heading: Working along one long side, * sc in next loop, ch 5. Repeat from * across, ending with sc in last loop. Break off.

Scalloped Edge: Attach thread to first loop on opposite side, sc in same loop, * ch 3, in next loop make (dc, ch 3, sc in 3rd ch from hook) 4 times and dc; ch 3, sc in next loop. Repeat from * across. Break off.

No. 8-60 Starting at narrow end, ch 9. **1st row:** 3 tr in 7th ch from hook, ch 1, skip 1 ch, tr in next ch. Ch 5, turn. **2nd row:** 3 tr in center tr of 3-tr group, ch 3, 7 tr in next loop. Ch 6, turn. **3rd row:** Skip first tr, (tr in next tr, ch 2) 5 times; tr in next tr, ch 5, 3 tr in center tr of 3-tr group, ch 1, skip 1 ch of turning chain below, tr in next ch. Ch 5, turn. **4th row:** 3 tr in center tr of 3-tr group, ch 7, holding back on hook the last loop of each tr make 3 tr in next ch-2 sp, thread over and draw through all loops on hook (cluster made); (ch 3, cluster in next sp) 5 times. Turn. **5th row:** * (Ch 5, sc in tip of cluster) 3 times; 3 sc in sp, sc in tip of cluster. Repeat from * 4 more times, (ch 5, sc in tip of cluster) 3 times; 6 sc in ch-7 sp, ch 5, 3 tr in center tr of 3-tr group, ch 1, skip 1 ch, tr in next ch. Ch 5, turn. Repeat 2nd to 5th rows incl for length desired. Break off.

Measure for Pleasure

Use Royal Society Cordichet, Sizes 30 and 50, with Steel Crochet Hooks Nos. 10 and 12.

No. 8-69 Make a chain slightly longer than length desired. **1st row:** Dc in 5th ch from hook, * ch 1, skip 1 ch, dc in next ch. Repeat from * across. Ch 1, turn. **2nd row:** Sc in first dc, sc in next sp, sc in next dc, * ch 3, skip next sp, 5 tr in next sp, ch 3, skip next sp, (sc in next dc, sc in next sp) twice; sc in next dc. Repeat from * across, ending with 3 sc. Ch 1, turn. **3rd row:** Sc in next sc, * ch 5, (dc in next tr, ch 2) 4 times; dc in next tr, ch 5, skip 2 sc, sc in next sc. Repeat from * across. Break off.

No. 8-70 Make a chain slightly longer than length desired. **1st row:** Sc in 2nd ch from hook, * ch 3, skip 2 ch, dc in next ch. ch 3, skip 2 ch, sc in next ch. Repeat from * across. Ch 1, turn. **2nd row:** 5 sc in each sp across. Ch 5, turn. **3rd row:** Skip 3 sc, * dc in next 4 sc, ch 5, skip 6 sc. Repeat from * across, ending with 4 dc, tr in last sc. Ch 3, turn. **4th row:** * Skip 1 dc, holding back on hook the last loop of each dc make dc in next 2 dc, thread over and draw through all loops on hook (cluster made); (ch 3, sc in 3rd ch from hook—picot made) twice; sc in next sp, 2 picots. Repeat from * across, ending with a cluster. Break off.

No. 8-71 Make a chain slightly longer than length desired. **1st row:** Dc in 5th ch from hook, * ch 1, skip 1 ch, dc in next ch. Repeat from * across. Ch 3, turn. **2nd row:** * Holding back on hook the last loop of each tr make 2 tr in next sp, thread over and draw through all loops on hook (cluster made), ch 6, dc in 6th ch from hook, (ch 5, dc in last dc) twice; cluster in same sp as last cluster was made, skip 3 sps. Repeat from * across. Break off.

No. 8-72 Make a chain slightly longer than length desired. **1st row:** Sc in 2nd ch from hook, * (ch 3, skip 1 ch, sc in next ch) 3 times; ch 1, skip 1 ch, dc in next ch, ch 3, turn; sc in next loop, ch 3, sc in next loop, ch 1, dc in next loop, ch 3, turn; sc in next loop, ch 1, dc in next loop, ch 3, turn; sc in next loop, ch 1, turn; sc in loop, (ch 5, sc in loop) 3 times; (ch 3, sc in 3rd ch from hook—picot made) 5 times; skip 3 ch (on starting chain), sc in next ch. Repeat from * across, ending with 5 picots and sc.

No. 8-73 Make a chain slightly longer than length desired. **1st row:** Dc in 4th ch from hook, * ch 2, skip 2 ch, dc in next 2 ch. Repeat from * across. Number of dc-groups should be divisible by 4 and 1 over. Ch 3, turn. **2nd row:** Skip first dc, dc in next dc, * ch 10, holding back on hook the last loop of each dc make dc in next 2 dc, thread over and draw through all loops on hook (cluster made); (cluster over next 2 dc) twice; ch 10, cluster over next 2 dc. Repeat from * across. Ch 1, turn. **3rd row:** * In next ch-10 loop make (3 sc, ch 5) 3 times and 3 sc; sc in tip of center cluster of the 3-cluster group, in next ch-10 loop make (3 sc, ch 5) 3 times and 3 sc. Repeat from * across. Break off.

8-69

8-70

8-71

8-72

8-73

Edgings-Go-Round

No. 8-95 Ch 9, make 5 dc in 9th ch from hook, ch 5, turn; * dc in next dc, ch 8, turn; 5 dc in last dc made, ch 5, turn. Repeat from * for length desired. Do not break off.

Heading: Work along side where the turning ch-5's appear as follows: * Dc in next ch-5 loop, ch 5. Repeat from * across. Break off.

Scalloped Edge: Attach thread to first ch-8 loop. In each ch-8 loop across make (3 sc, ch 3) 3 times and 3 sc. Break off.

No. 8-96 Make a chain slightly longer than length desired. **1st row:** Dc in 8th ch from hook, * ch 2, skip 2 ch, dc in next ch. Repeat from * across, having spaces divisible by 5 and 1 over. **2nd row:** Sc in sp, ch 5, * dc in next sp, (ch 2, dc in next sp) 3 times; ch 5, sc in next sp, ch 5. Repeat from * across, ending with ch 5, sc in sp. Ch 6, turn. **3rd row:** * Dc in next ch-2 sp, (ch 3, sc in 3rd ch from hook—picot made— dc in next sp) twice; ch 6, sc in next sc, ch 6. Repeat from * across. Break off.

No. 8-97 Make a chain slightly longer than length desired. **1st row:** Dc in 5th ch from hook, * ch 1, skip 1 ch, dc in next ch. Repeat from * across. Ch 4, turn. **2nd row:** Dc in next sp, * ch 3, thread over hook twice, insert hook in next sp and draw loop through, thread over and draw through 2 loops, thread over, skip next sp, insert hook in next sp and draw loop through, (thread over and draw through 2 loops) 4 times; ch 5, dc in center of cross (a cross st made), ch 3, dc in each of next 4 sps. Repeat from * across, ending with 2 dc. **3rd row:** * 3 sc in next ch-3 sp, sc in next st, 7 sc under next ch-5 sp, sc in next st, 3 sc in next ch-3 sp, sc in each of next 3 sps between dc's. Repeat from * across. Break off. **4th row:** Attach thread to first sc and, picking up only the back loop of each sc, make sc in next 4 sc, * (ch 5, sc in next 4 sc) twice; ch 5, sc in next 10 sc. Repeat from * across. Break off.

No. 8-98 Make a chain slightly longer than length desired. **1st row:** Sc in 2nd ch from hook and in each ch across, having number of sc divisible by 10 and 6 over. Ch 1, turn. **2nd row:** Sc in first sc, * ch 5, skip 4 sc, sc in next sc. Repeat from * across. Ch 4, turn. **3rd row:** Holding back on hook the last loop of each tr, make 3 tr in first loop, thread over and draw through all loops on hook (cluster made), * (ch 3, cluster in same loop) twice; skip next loop, make a cluster in next loop. Repeat from * across, ending with (cluster, ch 3) twice and cluster in last loop. Ch 11, turn. **4th row:** * Sc in next sp between 3-cluster groups, ch 11. Repeat from * across, ending with ch 11, sc in turning chain. Turn. **5th row:** In each loop across make 6 sc, ch 5 and 6 sc. Break off.

No. 8-99 **1st row:** Ch 15, sc in 6th ch from hook, (ch 3, skip 2 ch, sc in next ch) 3 times (4 loops). Ch 5, turn. **2nd row:** Sc in first sc, (ch 3, sc in next loop) 4 times. Ch 5, turn. **3rd row:** Sc in first loop, (ch 3, sc in next loop) 3 times. Ch 5, turn. Repeat 2nd and 3rd rows for length desired. Break off.

No. 8-100 Make a chain slightly longer than length desired. **1st row:** Sc in 2nd ch from hook and in each ch across. Ch 5, turn. **2nd row:** * Skip 1 sc, dc in next sc, ch 2. Repeat from * across. Turn. **3rd row:** Sl st in sp, ch 8, * skip 1 sp, dc in next sp, ch 5. Repeat from * across, ending with dc. Ch 3, turn. **4th row:** In each sp across make dc, ch 3 and dc. Turn. **5th row:** Sc in first dc, * ch 3, dc between next 2 dc, ch 3, sc in 3rd ch from hook (picot made), dc in same place as last dc. Repeat from * across. Break off.

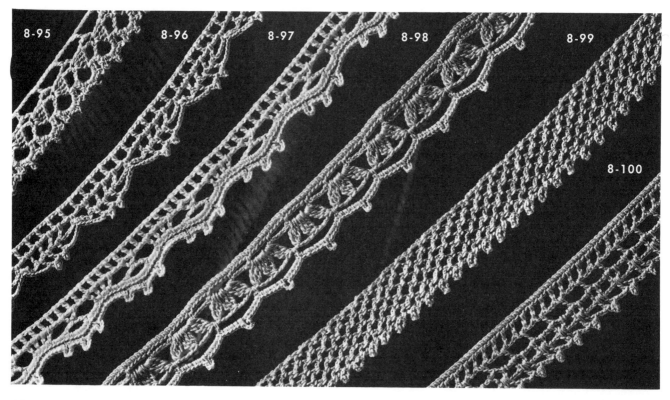

Tiny Treasures

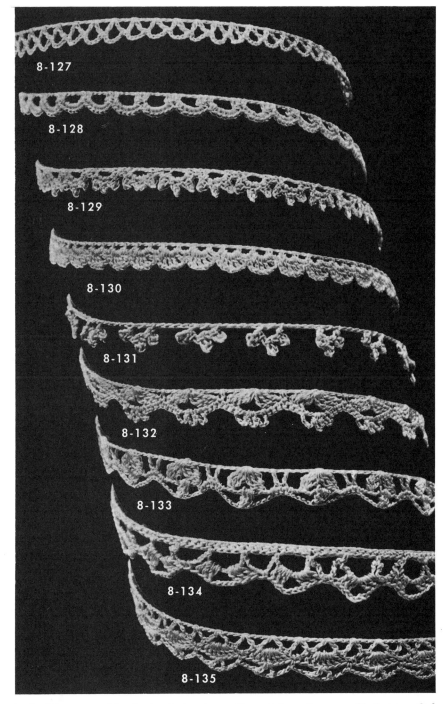

8-127
8-128
8-129
8-130
8-131
8-132
8-133
8-134
8-135

No. 8-127 Make a chain slightly longer than length desired. **1st row:** In 5th ch from hook make dc, ch 5 and dc; * skip 2 ch, in next ch make dc, ch 5 and dc. Repeat from * across. Break off.

No. 8-128 Make a chain slightly longer than length desired. **1st row:** Sc in 2nd ch from hook, sc in next 2 ch, * ch 5, skip 2 ch, sc in next 3 ch. Repeat from * across. **2nd row:** Make 7 sc in each loop across. Break off.

No. 8-129 **1st row:** Ch 5, dc in 5th ch from hook, * ch 8, dc in 5th ch from hook. Repeat from * for length desired. Ch 1, turn. **2nd row:** * Sc in next loop, ch 3, sc in 3rd ch from hook (picot made); in same loop make (sc, picot) twice and sc; skip 1 ch, sc in next ch. Repeat from * across. Break off.

No. 8-130 Make a chain slightly longer than length desired. **1st row:** Sc in 4th ch from hook, * ch 3, skip 1 ch, sc in next ch. Repeat from * across. Ch 1, turn. **2nd row:** Sc in first loop, * in next loop make (dc, ch 1) 4 times and dc; sc in next loop. Repeat from * across. Break off.

No. 8-131 (Ch 5, sc in 5th ch from hook—picot made) 3 times; dc in first ch made, * ch 5, make 3 picots, dc in 5th ch of previous ch-5. Repeat from * across. Break off.

No. 8-132 Make a chain slightly longer than length desired. **1st row:** 2 tr in 5th ch from hook, ch 5, 3 tr in same place, * skip 4 ch, sc in next ch, skip 4 ch, in next ch make 3 tr, ch 5 and 3 tr. Repeat from * across, ending with sc. **2nd row:** Sc in next 3 tr, * in next sp make (sc, ch 5) 3 times and sc; sc in next 6 tr. Repeat from * across. Break off.

No. 8-133 Make a chain slightly longer than length desired. **1st row:** Dc in 4th ch from hook, * ch 3, skip 3 ch, holding back on hook the last loop of each tr make 3 tr in next ch, thread over and draw through all loops on hook (cluster made), ch 4, cluster in same place as last cluster was made, ch 3, skip 3 ch, dc in next ch, skip 1 ch, dc in next ch. Repeat from * across, ending with cluster, ch 4 and cluster. Ch 5, turn. **2nd row:** * Make a 3-dc cluster in ch-4 sp between clusters, ch 5, sc in ch-3 sp, sc in next 2 dc, sc in next sp, ch 5. Repeat from * across. Break off.

No. 8-134 Make a chain slightly longer than length desired. **1st row:** Sc in 2nd ch from hook, sc in each ch across. Ch 1, turn. **2nd row:** Sc in first sc, * ch 9, skip 3 sc, sc in next sc. Repeat from * across. Ch 3, turn. **3rd row:** * In next loop make 3 dc, ch 5 and 3 dc; sc in next loop. Repeat from * across. Break off.

No. 8-135 Make a chain slightly longer than length desired. **1st row:** In 6th ch from hook make dc, ch 3 and dc; * skip 3 ch, in next ch make dc, ch 3 and dc. Repeat from * across. Ch 3, turn. **2nd row:** * Make 7 dc in next ch-3 sp, sc in next ch-3 sp. Repeat from * across. Ch 3, turn. **3rd row:** * In 4th dc of 7-dc group make dc, ch 3 and dc; ch 3, sc in next sc, ch 3. Repeat from * across. Break off.

Trimmings for Pillow Cases and Sheets

J. & P. Coats Big Ball Best Six Cord Mercerized Crochet, Art. A.104, or Clark's Big Ball Mercerized Crochet, Art. B.34: Use Size 30 with Milwards Steel Crochet Hook No. 10.

S-840 EDGING . . . Starting at narrow edge, ch 28. **1st row:** Dc in 8th ch from hook, dc in next 8 ch, ch 5, dc in next 9 ch, ch 2, skip 2 ch, dc in next ch. Ch 5, turn. **2nd row:** Skip first dc, dc in next 7 dc, ch 5, sc in next loop, ch 5, skip next 2 dc, dc in next 7 dc, ch 2, skip 2 ch, dc in next ch. Ch 5, turn. **3rd row:** Skip first dc, dc in next 5 dc, ch 5, sc in next loop, sc in next sc, sc in next loop, ch 5, skip next 2 dc, dc in next 5 dc, ch 2, skip 2 ch, dc in next ch. Ch 5, turn. **4th row:** Skip first dc, dc in next 3 dc, ch 5, sc in next loop, sc in next sc, ch 2, skip next sc, sc in next sc, sc in next loop, ch 5, skip next 2 dc, dc in next 3 dc, ch 2, skip 2 ch, dc in next ch. Ch 5, turn. **5th row:** Skip first dc, dc in next 3 dc, 2 dc in next loop, ch 5, skip next sc, sc in next sc, sc in ch-2 sp, sc in next sc, ch 5, 2 dc in next loop, dc in next 3 dc, ch 2, skip 2 ch, dc in next ch. Ch 5, turn. **6th row:** Skip first dc, dc in next 5 dc, 2 dc in next loop, ch 5, skip next sc, sc in next sc, ch 5, 2 dc in next loop, dc in next 5 dc, ch 2, skip 2 ch, dc in next ch. Ch 5, turn. **7th row:** Skip first dc, dc in next 7 dc, 2 dc in each of next 2 loops, dc in next 7 dc, ch 2, skip 2 ch, dc in next ch. Ch 5, turn. **8th row:** Skip first dc, dc in next 9 dc, ch 5, dc in next 9 dc, ch 2, skip 2 ch, dc in next ch. Ch 5, turn. Repeat 2nd to 8th rows incl until piece measures length desired, ending with 7th row. Do not break off, ch 1.

SCALLOPED EDGE . . . 1st row: Working across long side, make 3 sc in first 2 sps, * ch 5, skip next sp, (sc in next sp, ch 5) twice; skip next sp, 3 sc in each of next 3 sps. Repeat from * across, ending with ch 5, 3 sc in last sp. Ch 1, turn. **2nd row:** Sc in first sc, * ch 3, sc in next loop, ch 3, in next loop make (sc, ch 7 and sc); ch 3, sc in next loop, ch 3, skip next 2 sc, sc in next 5 sc. Repeat from * across, ending with sc in last 4 sc. Ch 1,

turn. **3rd row:** Sc in first sc, * ch 3, in ch-7 loop make (tr, ch 3) 7 times; sc in center sc of next 5-sc group. Repeat from * across, ending with sc in last sc. Break off.

INSERTION . . . Work exactly as for Edging, omitting Scalloped Edge.

S-841 EDGING—First Motif . . . Starting at center, ch 10. Join with sl st to form a ring. **1st rnd:** Working over a strand of "Speed-Cro-Sheen," make 20 sc in ring. Join. Cut off "Speed-Cro-Sheen." **2nd rnd:** Ch 4, * dc in next sc, ch 1. Repeat from * around. Join last ch-1 with sl st to 3rd ch of ch-4. **3rd rnd:** Ch 1, working over a strand of "Speed-Cro-Sheen" make 2 sc in each ch-1 sp around. Join. Cut off "Speed-Cro-Sheen." **4th rnd:** Ch 5, * skip 1 sc, dc in next sc, ch 2. Repeat from * around. Join last ch-2 to 3rd ch of ch-5. **5th rnd:** Working over a strand of "Speed-Cro-Sheen," make * 2 sc in next sp, ch 3, sl st in last sc (picot), 2 sc in same sp. Repeat from * around. Join. Break off.

SECOND MOTIF . . . Work as for First Motif until 4 rnds have been completed. **5th rnd:** Working over a strand of "Speed-Cro-Sheen" make 2 sc in next loop, ch 1, sl st in any picot of First Motif, ch 1, sl st in last sc of Second Motif, 2 sc in same loop, join next loop in the same way and complete rnd as for First Motif.

Make the necessary number of motifs for length desired, joining other motifs as Second Motif was joined to First Motif leaving 8 free picots on each side of joining.

HEADING . . . 1st row: Attach thread to 8th free picot on last motif to the right of joining, ch 7, * tr in next picot, ch 2, dc in next picot, (ch 2, half dc in next picot) twice; ch 2, dc in next picot, ch 2, tr in next picot, (ch 2, d tr in next picot) twice; ch 2. Repeat from * across, ending to cor-

respond with beginning. Ch 1, turn. **2nd row:** Working over a strand of "Speed-Cro-Sheen," in each loop across make 2 sc, picot and 2 sc. Break off.

INSERTION . . . Work as for Edging, making Heading on both sides of motifs.

S-842 With White, ch 6, d tr in 6th ch from hook, * ch 5, d tr in last d tr made. Repeat from * across until row measures slightly longer than length desired, having an uneven number of loops. Now work across long side as follows: **1st row:** Ch 5, in first loop make (tr, ch 1) 6 times; * sc in next loop, ch 1, in next loop make (tr, ch 1) 7 times. Repeat from * across to within last loop, in last loop make (tr, ch 1) 14 times; working across opposite side, sc in next loop and complete row to correspond, ending with (tr, ch 1) 7 times in last loop, sl st in 4th ch of starting ch-5.

SCALLOPED EDGE . . . 1st row: Ch 4, * (dc in next tr, ch 1) twice; in next tr make (dc, ch 1) 3 times; (dc in next tr, ch 1) twice; dc in next 2 tr, ch 1. Repeat from * across, ending with dc in 7th tr of last scallop. Break off. **2nd row:** Attach White to first sp, * (ch 3, sc in next sp) 7 times; sc in next sp. Repeat from * across to within last scallop, (ch 3, sc in next sp) 6 times; ch 1, half dc in last sp. Ch 3, turn. **3rd row:** * (Sc in next loop, ch 3) twice; in next loop make sc, ch 3, sc, (ch 3, sc in next loop) 3 times; sc in next loop, ch 3. Repeat from * across. Break off and turn. **4th row:** Attach Beauty Rose to first ch-3 loop, * (ch 3, sc in next loop) twice; ch 3, in next loop make sc, ch 3 and sc; (ch 3, sc in next loop) 3 times; sc in next loop. Repeat from * across. Turn. **5th row:** Sl st in first ch-3 loop, * (ch 3, sc in next loop) twice; ch 3, holding back

Continued on page 40.

S-840

S-841

S-842

**Give a custom-made look
of luxury to your bedroom**

S-843

S-844

S-845

**Motif measures 3¾ inches
from point to point.**

S-843 FIRST MOTIF . . . Starting at center with Size 30, ch 8. Join with sl st to form ring. **1st rnd:** Working over a strand of "Speed-Cro-Sheen," make 20 sc in ring. Join with sl st to first sc. Cut off "Speed-Cro-Sheen." **2nd rnd:** Ch 4, * dc in next sc, ch 1. Repeat from * around. Join to 3rd ch of ch-4. **3rd rnd:** Working over a strand of "Speed-Cro-Sheen," make sc in same place as sl st, * 2 sc in next sp, sc in next dc. Repeat from * around. Join. Cut off "Speed-Cro-Sheen." **4th rnd:** Sc in same place as sl st, * ch 5, skip 2 sc, sc in next sc. Repeat from * around. Join (20 loops). **5th and 6th rnds:** Sl st to center of next loop, sc in same loop, * ch 5, sc in next loop. Repeat from * around. Join. Break off at end of 6th rnd. **7th rnd:** Ch 15, drop loop from hook, insert hook in any loop on last rnd, draw dropped loop through, * make 5 sc, ch 3 and 5 sc over bar of ch 15, ch 15, drop loop from hook and, working from left to right, insert hook in loop preceding last loop worked, draw dropped loop through. Repeat from * around, ending with 5 sc, ch 3 and 5 sc over last ch-15 bar, drop loop from hook, insert hook in first loop of starting chain, draw dropped loop through, thus joining rnd. **8th rnd:** 9 sc in first sp, * 5 sc in next sp, ch 12, drop loop from hook, insert hook in center sc of 9-sc group, draw dropped

Continued on page 40.

S-842 .. Continued from page 38.

on hook the last loop of each dc make 2 dc in next loop, thread over and draw through all loops on hook (a dc cluster made); ch 5, dc in 4th ch from hook, make another dc cluster in same loop, (ch 3, sc in next loop) 3 times; sc in next loop. Repeat from * across. Break off.

HEADING . . . 1st row: Attach White to the 2nd free sp on opposite side of edging, ch 6, * skip next sp, (sc in next sp, ch 3) twice; skip next sp, holding back on hook the last loop of each dc, make dc in next sp, skip next 2 sps, dc in next sp, thread over and draw through all loops on hook (a joint dc made), ch 3. Repeat from * across, ending with dc. Ch 1, turn. **2nd row:** Sc in first sp, * ch 3, sc in next sp. Repeat from * across. Ch 5, turn. **3rd row:** Dc in next sp, * ch 2, dc in next sp. Repeat from * across. Break off.

S-843 .. Continued from page 39.

loop through, 12 sc in loop just formed, ch 8, drop loop from hook, insert hook in 6th sc of 12-sc group, draw dropped loop through, in loop just formed make 5 sc, ch 3 and 5 sc; 5 sc in next incompleted loop, 4 sc in next incompleted sp, 9 sc in next sp. Repeat from * until 6 points have been completed, ending with 4 sc in last incompleted sp, make 5 sc, ch 3 and 5 sc in each remaining sp around. Join and break off.

SECOND MOTIF . . . Work as for First Motif until 7 rnds have been completed. **8th rnd:** 9 sc in first sp, * 5 sc in next sp, ch 12, drop loop from hook, insert hook in center sc of 9-sc group, draw dropped loop through, 12 sc in loop just formed, ch 8, drop loop from hook, insert hook in 6th sc of 12-sc group, draw dropped loop through, 5 sc in loop just formed, ch 1, sl st in ch-3 loop of last point made on First Motif, ch 1, 5 sc in same loop on Second Motif. Complete as for First Motif (no more joinings).

Make necessary number of motifs, joining as Second Motif was joined to First Motif.

Motif measures 2¾ inches square

Illustrated on Page 39.

S-844 FIRST MOTIF . . .

Starting at center, ch 4. **1st rnd:** 23 dc in 4th ch from hook. Join with sl st to top of starting chain. **2nd rnd:** Sc in same place as sl st, * ch 3, skip next dc, sc in next dc. Repeat from * around. Join to first sc (12 loops). **3rd rnd:** Sl st to center of next loop, sc in same loop, (ch 5, sc in next loop) twice; * ch 5, sc in same loop as last sc was made (corner loop made), (ch 5, sc in next loop) 3 times. Repeat from * around, ending with ch 2, dc in first sc. **4th rnd:** Sl st in loop just formed, ch 3, holding back on hook the last loop of each dc, make 2 dc in same loop, thread over and draw through all loops on hook (cluster made); (ch 2, make 3-dc cluster in next loop) twice; * ch 2, in next corner loop make 3-dc cluster, ch 5 and 3-dc cluster; (ch 2, cluster in next loop) 3 times. Repeat from * around. Join to tip of first cluster. **5th rnd:** Sl st in next sp, sc in same sp, (ch 5, sc in next sp) 3 times; * ch 5, sc in same sp as last sc was made, (ch 5, sc in next sp) 5 times. Repeat from * around, ending with ch 2, dc in first sc. **6th rnd:** Sc in loop just formed, * ch 5, sc in next loop. Repeat from * around. Join to first sc. **7th rnd:** Sl st to center of next loop, sc in same loop, * ch 5, sc in next loop, ch 13, skip next 2 sc, sc in next sc, ch 13, skip next 2 loops, sc in next loop. Repeat from * around. Join. **8th rnd:** Sl st in next loop, ch 8, in same loop make (d tr, ch 3) 5 times and d tr; * ch 7, skip next sp, sc in next sc, ch 7, in next ch-5 loop make (d tr, ch 5) 6 times and d tr. Repeat from * around. Join to 5th ch of ch-8. **9th rnd:** Sc in same place as sl st, * (3 sc in next sp, sc in next d tr) 3 times; ch 3, sc in same d tr as last sc was made, (3 sc in next sp, sc in next d tr) 3 times; 8 sc in next sp, sc in next sc, 8 sc in next sp, sc in next d tr. Repeat from * around. Join and break off.

SECOND MOTIF . . . Work as for First Motif until 8 rnds have been completed. **9th rnd:** Sc in same place as sl st, (3 sc in next sp, sc in next d tr) 3 times; ch 1, sl st in any corner loop on First Motif, ch 1, sc in same d tr on Second Motif. Complete rnd as for First Motif (no more joinings).

Make necessary number of motifs, joining as Second Motif was joined to First Motif, leaving 1 corner free on each side of joining.

Motif measures 3 inches in diameter

Illustrated on Page 39.

S-845 FIRST MOTIF . . .

Starting at center with White, ch 10. Join with sl st to form ring. **1st rnd:** Ch 3, 31 dc in ring. Join. **2nd rnd:** Ch 5, * skip 1 dc, dc in next dc, ch 2. Repeat from * around. Join to 3rd ch of ch-5 (16 sps). **3rd rnd:** * Ch 5, 2 d tr in next sp, d tr in next dc, 2 d tr in next sp, ch 5, sl st in next dc. Repeat from * around. Join. **4th rnd:** Sl st in next 5 ch, ch 5, holding back on hook the last loop of each d tr make a d tr in each d tr and in top of next ch, thread over and draw through all loops on hook (cluster made), * ch 15, make a cluster by making d tr in top of next ch, in each d tr and in top of next ch. Repeat from * around. Join. **5th rnd:** Make 18 sc in each sp around. Join to first sc. **6th rnd:** Sc in same place as sl st, sc in next 2 sc, * (ch 3, sc in 3rd ch from hook—picot made—sc in next 3 sc) 5 times; sc in next 3 sc. Repeat from * around. Join and break off.

ROSETTE . . . 1st rnd: Attach Mid Rose to any free dc on first rnd, sc in same place, * ch 3, sc in next free dc. Repeat from * around. Join to first sc. **2nd rnd:** Sl st to center of first loop, sc in same loop, * 5 dc in next loop, sc in next loop. Repeat from * around. Join and break off.

SECOND MOTIF . . . Work as for First Motif until 5 rnds have been completed. **6th rnd:** Sc in same place as sl st, sc in next 2 sc, picot, sc in next 3 sc, (ch 1, sl st in corresponding picot on First Motif, ch 1, sc in first ch made on Second Motif, sc in next 3 sc) 3 times; picot, sc in next 3 sc. Complete rnd (no more joinings). Make Rosette in center as before.

Make necessary number of motifs, joining as Second Motif was joined to First Motif, leaving 3 loops free on each side of joining.

More Handkerchief Edgings

No. 19—HANDKERCHIEF EDGE

WIDTH—⅝ inch.

MATERIALS—Lily SIX CORD Mercerized Crochet Cotton, size 40.

Join thread ⅛-inch to right of one corner and working closely over rolled edge of handkerchief, make 1 sc, ch 5, 2 dc in 5th st from hook, holding the last loop of each dc on hook, thread over and pull thru all 3 loops on hook at once (a Cluster), ch 5, sl st in Cluster for a p, ch 4, sl st at base of Cluster (a Cluster-petal), 2 sc in corner, make another Cluster-petal, 2 sc, another Cluster-petal, (8 sc, a Cluster-petal) repeated around, making 3 Cluster-petals separated by 2 sc at each corner. Make an uneven number of Cluster-petals on each side between the triple-groups at each corner. Fasten off. **ROW 2**—Join to tip of 1st Cluster-petal, ch 3, 8 dc in same place, (9 dc in next Cluster-petal) repeated around. Sl st in 1st 3-ch, sl st in next 4 dc. **ROW 3**—Ch 4, dc in center dc of next (corner) shell, (ch 5, sc in 5th st from hook for a p, ch 1, dc in same dc) 5 times, * ch 4, sc in next shell, ch 4, dc in next shell, (ch 5, p, ch 1, dc in same place) 3 times. Repeat from * around, making each corner like 1st one. Fasten off.

No. 20—HANDKERCHIEF EDGE

WIDTH—¾ inch.

MATERIALS—Lily SIX CORD Mercerized Crochet Cotton, size 40.

Finish edge of linen with a rolled hem.

Join to one corner, ch 5, sc in same corner, (ch 5, sc about ⅛-inch away) repeated around, making each corner like 1st

one. **ROW 2**—Ch 1, sl st in 1st loop, * ch 27, remove hook, insert it in 12th st from hook, catch loop and pull thru, forming a ring, ch 1, (4 sc in ring, ch 5, sl st in last sc for a p) * 3 times, 4 sc in bal. of ring, 16 sc over 13 of next 15 ch sts, ch 2, sc in same corner loop, ** (ch 5, sc in next loop) twice. Repeat from * to *. 4 sc in ring, ch 2, and fasten back with a sl st in 8th sc up last scroll, ch 2, sl st back in last sc, (4 sc, a p and 4 sc) in bal. of ring, 16 sc over 13 of next 15 ch sts, ch 2, sc in next loop. Repeat from ** around, putting scrolls closer together around corners. Fasten off.

No. 21—HANDKERCHIEF EDGE

WIDTH—1 inch.

MATERIALS—Lily SIX CORD Mercerized Crochet Cotton, size 40.

Finish edge of linen with a rolled hem. Join to one corner, ** (ch 5, sc ⅛-inch away) 6 times, ch 2, dc ⅛-inch away. * Turn, (ch 5, sc in next loop) repeated to 2nd loop from end, ch 2, dc in next (end) loop. Repeat from * 4 times. Ch 5, turn, sc in next loop. Cut thread 2 inches from work and pull thru loop, tight. Join to edge of linen in same place with last sc and repeat from ** around. **ROW 2**—Join to one corner of linen, between points, sc in 1st space on point, (3 sc in next) 6 times, ch 5, sl st in last sc for a p, * 3 sc in same end space, (3 sc in next) 5 times, 1 sc in next, 1 sc in 1st space on next point, (3 sc in next) 3 times, 2 sc in next, ch 11, turn, sl st in 12th sc up side of last point, ch 1, turn, 13 sc over 11-ch, 1 sc in same space on point, ch 6, turn, dc in center sc on bar, ch 8, dc in same st, ch 6, sl st in next sc on point, ch 1, turn, 6 sc over 6-ch, (5 sc, a p and 5 sc) over 8-ch, (6 sc, 1 sl st and ch 1) over next 6-ch, (3 sc over next space on point) twice, a p. Repeat from * to next corner, 1 sc in corner of linen, 1 sc in 1st space on next point, (3 sc in next space) 3 times, 2 sc over next, ch 11, turn, dtr down into corner sc in linen, ch 11, dtr in same st, ch 11, sl st in 12th sc up side of next point, ch 1, turn, 13 sc over each 11-ch. 1 sc in each dtr, 1 sc in same space on point, turn, (ch 6, dc in next 7th sc on corner bar, ch 8, dc in same st, ch 6, sc in next 7th sc) 3 times, ch 1, turn, (6 sc over 6-ch, 5 sc, a p and 5 sc over 8-ch, 6 sc over 6-ch) 3 times, (3 sc in next space on point) twice, a p. Repeat from * around. Make final corner like others.

No. 22—HANDKERCHIEF EDGE

WIDTH—¾ inch.

MATERIALS—Lily SIX CORD Mercerized Crochet Cotton, size 40.

Finish edge of linen with a rolled hem.

Join to one corner, (ch 6, sc in 5th st from hook for a p) 4 times, ch 1, hdc in 1-ch between 3d and 4th ps from hook, ch 5, sc in 5th st from hook for a p, sk next p, dc in next 1-ch, ch 1, sc in same corner, 2 more sc in hem. * Make another p-loop, sk about 3/16-inch, then make 3 sc in hem. Repeat from * around, making each corner like 1st one. Make an uneven number of p-loops on each side between corner p-loops. Fasten off. **ROW 2**—Join to 1st p-loop to right of one corner, ch 1, dtr in corner loop, (ch 2, tr in same place) 7 times, ch 2, dtr in same place, ch 1, sc in next p-loop. * ch 1, tr in next loop, (ch 2, tr in same loop) 6 times, ch 1, sc in next loop. Repeat from * around, making each corner shell like 1st one. **ROW 3**—Sl st to 2-ch between 1st dtr and tr, (ch 5, sc in next 2-ch space) 7 times, * ch 3, sc between 1st 2 tr of next shell, (ch 5, sc in next 2-ch space) 5 times. Repeat from * around, making corners like 1st one. Fasten off.

1859
1860
1861
1862

Trousseau Edgings

THAT WILL SERVE AS HEIRLOOM TREASURES

USE AMERICAN THREAD COMPANY "STAR" or "GEM"
MERCERIZED CROCHET COTTON
Sizes 10 to 50

No. 1859

Work a row of s c working 2 s c in every 3rd s c.

2nd Row. Starting in 3rd s c from inside corner, work 1 s c, ch 2, skip 1 s c, s c in next s c, ch 2, skip 1 s c, short double crochet in next s c, * ch 2, skip 1 s c, d c in next s c, repeat from * twice, * ch 2, skip 1 s c, tr c in next s c, repeat from * to the 13th st from end of scallop, complete scallop same as the beginning and continue all around.

3rd Row. Work 3 s c in each of the 1st 5 meshes, * ch 4, turn, skip 2 s c, sl st in next s c, ch 1, turn and work 3 s c, ch 3, 3 s c over loop, 3 s c in each of the next 2 meshes and repeat from * to the last 4 meshes of scallop, 3 s c over the 4 meshes on scallop, corner mesh and 1 mesh on next scallop, ch 4, turn, sl st over the s d c of 1st scallop, ch 1, turn and work 3 s c, ch 3, 3 s c over loop and continue all around.

No. 1860

Work a row of s c working 2 s c in every 3rd s c.

2nd Row. Ch 3, skip 2 s c, d c in next s c, ch 3, d c in same space, * skip 2 s c, d c in next s c, ch 3, d c in same s c, repeat from * all around.

3rd Row. 2 s c in each mesh and 1 s c in each d c.

4th Row. * Ch 3, skip 2 s c, d c in next s c, ch 3, d c in same space, ch 3, skip 2 s c, s c in next s c, repeat from * all around.

No. 1861

Work a row of s c working 2 s c in every 3rd space.

2nd Row. Ch 6, skip 3 s c, sl st in next s c, repeat all around always ending a loop in inside corner.

3rd Row. Sl st to 3rd st of loop, ch 3, 2 d c in same space, ch 3, 3 d c in next st of loop, * ch 2, 1 d c over next loop, ch 2, 3 d c in 3rd st of next loop, ch 3, 3 d c in next st of loop, repeat from * to last loop of scallop, if pattern ends with a d c, start next scallop with a d c omitting the chs between. If pattern ends with shell start next scallop with a shell.

No. 1862

Work a row of s c working 2 s c in every 3rd space.

2nd Row. Ch 3, d c in next s c, * ch 2, skip 1 s c, 1 d c in each of the next 2 s c, repeat from * all around.

3rd Row. * 2 s c over mesh, s c in d c, ch 4, sl st in 1st stitch for picot, s c in next d c, repeat from * to the 3rd group of d c from inside corner, continue s c without picot over the next 5 meshes, ch 4, turn, 1 d c over each of the next 2 d c, ch 7, skip 2 groups of d c, 1 d c in each of the next 2 d c, ch 4, sl st over next group of d c, ch 1, turn, 6 s c over 4 ch loop, ch 2 and over 7 ch loop work 4 d c, picot, 4 d c, picot, 4 d c, ch 2, 6 s c over 4 ch loop and continue all around.

No. 1863

Work 1 d c in each space of hemstitching or ch for desired length.

2nd Row. 1 s c in each of the next 9 d c, * ch 3, skip 2 d c, 1 d c in each of the next 2 d c, ch 3, skip 2 d c, 1 s c in each of the next 9 d c, repeat from *.

3rd Row. Skip 1st s c, 1 s c in each of the next 7 s c * ch 3, 2 d c in next loop, ch 3, 2 d c in next loop, ch 3, skip 1st s c, 1 s c in each of the next 7 s c, and repeat from *.

4th Row. 1 s c in each of the center 5 s c, * ch 3, 2 d c in next loop, repeat from * twice, ch 3 and repeat from beginning.

5th Row. 1 s c in each of the center 3 s c, * ch 3, 2 d c in next loop, repeat from * 3 times, ch 3 and repeat from beginning.

6th Row. Same as 5th row having 1 s c in center of s c group and 2 d c in each loop with ch 3 between.

7th Row. S c in 1st loop, 1 s d c, 2 d c, 1 s d c in next loop, * s c in next loop, 1 s d c, 2 d c, 1 s d c in same loop, repeat from * twice, s c in next loop, s c in s c of previous row, s c in next loop, 1 s d c, 2 d c, 1 s d c in same loop and repeat across row.

No. 1864

Work 1 s c in each space of hemstitching or ch for desired length.

2nd Row. * Ch 5, skip 2 sts, s c in next st, repeat from * across row.

3rd Row. Sl st to center of loop, * ch 5, s c in next loop, repeat from * across row.

4th Row. Sl st to center of loop, ch 3, d c in next loop, ch 3, cluster st in next loop, (cluster st, thread over twice, insert in loop, pull through, thread over, pull through 2 loops, thread over, pull through next 2 loops, thread over twice, insert in same space, pull through, thread over, pull through 2 loops, thread over, pull through next 2 loops, thread over, insert in same loop, pull through, * thread over, pull through 2 loops, repeat from*, thread over and pull through all loops on needle) ch 4, cluster st in same loop, * ch 3, d c in next loop, d c in next loop, ch 3, 2 cluster sts with ch 4 between in next loop and repeat from * across row.

5th Row. Sl st to center ch between clusters, 5—2 tr c cluster sts in same space with ch 2 between each cluster st, * ch 2, d c between the two d c of previous row, ch 2, skip next loop, 5 cluster sts with ch 2 between each cluster in next loop and repeat from *.

6th Row. Ch 3, s c in ch between cluster sts, * ch 3, s c in next ch, repeat from * twice, ch 3, s c in d c of previous row, ch 3, s c between next 2 cluster sts and repeat from beginning.

No. 1865

Ch for desired length, d c in 8th st from hook, * ch 2, skip 2 sts, d c in next st, repeat from * to end of row.

2nd Row. Ch 3, 3 d c in 1st mesh, ch 2, skip 1 mesh, 4 d c in next mesh, * ch 5, skip 1 mesh, s c in next mesh, ch 5, skip 1 mesh, 4 d c in next mesh, ch 2, skip 1 mesh, 4 d c in next mesh, repeat from *.

3rd Row. Ch 5, 4 d c in next mesh, ch 2, 4 d c in next mesh, * ch 5, 4 d c in next mesh, ch 2, 4 d c in next mesh, ch 2, 4 d c in next mesh, repeat from * ending row with ch 2, d c in last d c.

4th Row. Ch 3, 3 d c in 1st mesh, ch 2, 4 d c in next mesh, * ch 5, s c over next mesh, ch 5, 4 d c in next mesh, ch 2, 4 d c in next mesh, repeat from *.

5th Row. Ch 5, 4 d c in next loop, * ch 7, sl st in 5th st from hook for picot, ch 7, sl st in 5th st from hook for picot, ch 2, s c over next loop, ch 7, sl st in 5th st from hook for picot, ch 2, s c in next loop, double picot loop, 4 d c in next loop, repeat from *.

Filet Edgings and Insertions

No. 56 EDGING

WIDTH—2⅛ inches.

MATERIALS— Lily SIX CORD Mercerized Crochet Cotton, size 40.

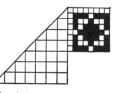

Start here

GIANT FILET POINT—Ch 54, * tr in 18th st from hook, (ch 5, tr in next 6th st) 4 times, ch 5, tr in next 6th st, dtr in next 6th (end) st, holding the last loop of these 2 sts on hook, thread over and pull thru all 3 loops on hook at once (a Cluster). **ROW 2**—Ch 8, turn, sk Cluster, tr in next tr, (ch 5, tr in next tr) 4 times, ch 5, tr in 6th st of end ch. **ROW 3**—Ch 11, turn, tr in next tr, (ch 5, tr in next tr) twice, ch 5, (tr in next tr, dtr in end Cluster) made into a Cluster. Continue, following diagram, for 3 more rows. **ROW 7**—Ch 5, turn, dtr in end Cluster.

FILET SQUARE—Ch 5, turn, dc in 3d st of previous 5-ch space, ch 2, dc in next 3d st, ch 2, dc in center of next tr, ch 2, dc in next row (4 sps made). Continue, making 4 more spaces. Ch 3, turn, (2 dc in 2-ch sp, dc in dc) 3 times (3 bls made), 1 sp, 3 bls, 1 sp. Ch 5, turn, dc in next 4 dc, (2 sps, 1 bl) twice. Continue for 5 more rows, following diagram. Ch 29 and repeat from * for desired length.

Work across top of lace with 8 sc in each space. **ROW 2**—Ch 5, turn, dc in next 3d st, (ch 2, dc in next 3d st) repeated across. Fasten off.

EDGE—Join to starting st, ch 5, dc in next 3d st, (ch 2, dc in next 3d st) 13 times to corner st, * ch 5, dc in same corner, 5 sps, sk 5 sts in angle, dc in next st, 7 sps to corner, ch 5, dc in same corner, 7 sps, dc in center of next Giant Filet sp, 5 sps. Repeat from * around. Fasten off. **ROW 2**—Join to 1st 5-ch of last row, 3 sc in 1st 3 sps, * (2 sc, ch 5, sl st in last sc for a p, and 1 sc) in next sp, 3 sc in next 2 sps. Repeat from * twice. (2 sc, a p and 1 sc) in next sp, 3 sc in next, (3 sc, a p and 3 sc) in corner sp, 3 sc in next, (2 sc, a p and 1 sc) in next, 3 sc in next 5 sps, (2 sc, a p and 1 sc) in next space. Continue, working around with sc, putting 5 ps around each Filet Square point, and 3 ps around each Giant Filet point.

FLOWER—(Ch 6, a 2-tr-Cluster in 6th st from hook, a 5-ch p, ch 6, sl st at base of Cluster) 4 times, sl st in starting st. Fasten off. Sew a Flower in center of each Giant Filet point.

No. 57 BANDING

Start here

WIDTH—1⅛ inches.

MATERIALS—Lily SIX CORD Mercerized Crochet Cotton, size 40.

Ch 27, dc in 9th st from hook, (ch 2, dc in next 3d st) twice, dc in next 3 sts, (ch 2, dc in next 3d st) 3 times (3 sps, 1 bl and 3 sps made). **ROW 2**—Ch 5, turn, dc in next dc, 2 sps, 1 bl and 3 sps. Repeat this row 4 times. **ROW 7**—2 sps, 1 bl, 1 sp, 1 bl and 2 sps. **ROW 8**—1 sp, 1 bl, ch 4, dc in center space, ch 4, sk 3 dc, 1 bl, 1 sp. **ROW 9**—Ch 3, turn, 1 bl, ch 6, dc in left end of next 4-ch, dc in center dc, dc in next 4-ch, ch 6, sk 3 dc, 1 bl. **ROW 10**—1 sp, 1 bl, ch 3, dc in center dc, ch 3, 1 bl, 1 sp. **ROW 11**—2 sps, 1 bl, 1 sp, 1 bl and 2 sps. Repeat Row 2 six times, then repeat from Row 7 for desired length.

EDGE—Join to 1st sp, (ch 4, sl st in same sp, ch 1, sl st in next sp) repeated on both sides of lace.

No. 58 EDGING

WIDTH—3 inches.

MATERIALS—Lily SIX CORD Mercerized Crochet Cotton, size 40.

Ch 64, sk last 4 sts, dc in next 57 sts, ch 2, dc in next 3d (end) st. **ROW 2**—Ch 5, turn, dc in next 4 dc, (ch 2, dc in next 3d dc) 16 times (1 sp, 1 bl and 16 sps made). **ROW 3**—Ch 3, turn, (2 dc in next space, dc in next dc) 15 times, 1 sp, 1 bl and 1 sp. Continue, following diagram, for 4 more

Start here

rows. **ROW 8**—Ch 5 turning sp, (1 bl, 1 sp) 4 times, (ch 5, dc in next 6th st) twice, 1 sp. **ROW 9**—Ch 6, turn, sk last 4 sts, dc in next 3 sts (an added bl), (ch 5, dc in 3d st of next 5-ch sp) twice, ch 5, sk next 5 sts, (1 bl, 1 sp) 4 times. **ROW 10**—Ch 5 turning sp, (1 bl, 1 sp) 4 times, (ch 5, dc in 3d st of next 5-ch sp) twice, 1 sp, 1 bl. Continue, following diagram, for desired length. To add 2 extra bls, as in Rows 33, 35 and 37, ch 9, sk last 4 sts, dc in remaining 5 sts, dc in next dc.

CORNER—Add 2 extra bls, then work solid dc to end of row. Fasten off. Without turning, join to 7th dc from end of this last row, ch 57, sk last 4 sts, dc in each remaining st, sk 2 dc of last row, sl st in remaining 4 dc. Turn, 16 sps. Ch 3, turn, 15 bls, 1 sp, 1 bl and 1 sp. Repeat from Row 4 for desired length. To fill out Corner, join to 7th st from end of 1 point, ch 5, dc in next 3d st, 13 sps, ch 2, dc in next 3d st, dc across corner in 3d st on next side, making these 2 dc into a Cluster, 15 sps. Ch 3, turn, 13 bls, 2 dc in next space, (dc in next dc, dc in next sp, dc in Cluster, dc in sp, dc in next dc) making

these 5 dc into a Cluster, 14 bls. Ch 1, turn, sk last dc, sl st in next 6 dc, 10 sps and continue, following diagram for this and 3 more rows. Then ch 1, turn, sk last dc, sl st in next 6 dc, 1 sp, ch 5, (dc in next 6th dc, dc in next 6th dc) made into a Cluster, ch 5, dc in next 6th dc, 1 sp. Ch 3, turn, 1 bl, ch 3, 1 bl in end sp of last row. Ch 1, turn, sk last dc, sl st in next 3 dc, ch 2, 4 dc over 3-ch, ch 2, sl st in next dc. Fasten off.

No. 59—EDGING

Start here

WIDTH—1⅜ inches.

MATERIALS—Lily SIX CORD Mercerized Crochet Cotton, size 40.

Ch 24, sk last 8 sts, dc in next 13 sts, ch 2, dc in next 3d (end) st. **ROW 2**—Ch 3, turn, 2 dc in sp, dc in next dc, (ch 5, dc in next 6th dc) twice, 3 dc in sp. **ROW 3**—Ch 6, turn, sk last 4 sts, dc in next 3 sts, for an added bl, (ch 5, dc in 3d st of next 5-ch sp) twice, 2 dc over next 2-ch, dc in 4 dc. **ROW 4**—Ch 3, turn, dc in next 6 dc, 3 dc over next 5-ch, ch 5, dc in 3d st of next 5-ch, ch 8, sl st in next 6th st, ch 3, turn, 3 dc over 8-ch. **ROW 5**—Make an added bl as in Row 3, (ch 5, dc in 3d st of next 5-ch) twice, 3 bls, 1 sp. **ROW 6**—Turn, 2 sps, 1 bl, 1 sp, (5 dc over next 5-ch) twice, ch 5, sl st in next 3d st, ch 5, sc in 5th st from hook for a p, ch 1, turn, sl st in 3d st of 5-ch. **ROW 7**—Ch 3, 2 dc over bal. of 5-ch, dc in dc, (ch 5, dc in next 6th st) twice, 3 bls, 1 sp. **ROW 8**—Ch 3, turn, 3 bls, (ch 5, dc in 3d st of next 5-ch space) twice, 2 dc over next 2-ch, dc in dc. **ROW 9**—Ch 1, turn, sk last dc, sl st in next 3 dc, ch 3, 3 dc over next 5-ch, ch 5, dc in center of next 5-ch space, ch 5, sk 3 dc, 2 bls. Continue, following diagram, for desired length.

No. 60—EDGING

Start here

WIDTH—¾ inch.

MATERIALS—Lily SIX CORD Mercerized Crochet Cotton, size 40.

Ch 18, dc in 15th st from hook, ch 2, dc in next 3d (end) st. **ROW 2**—Ch 8, turn, sk last 2 dc, dc in next 3d st, 3 dc over next ch. **ROW 3**—Ch 6, turn, sk last 4 sts, dc in next 3 sts, ch 2, dc in next 3d dc, 3 dc over next 8-ch, ch 2, dc in 3d st from left end of same ch. **ROW 4**—Ch 8, turn, sk last 4 dc, dc in next

dc, 2 dc in next 2-ch space, dc in next dc. **ROW 5**—Ch 8, turn, sk last 4 dc, dc in next 3d ch st, ch 2, dc in next 3d st. **ROW 6**—Ch 8, turn, sk last 2 dc, dc in next 3d ch st, ch 2, dc in next 3d st. Repeat this row once. Repeat from Row 2 for desired length. Fasten off.

EDGE—Join to 1st Row with 2 sc, * ch 7, sc in 5th st from hook for a p, ch 3, sc in end point of next 2d row, ch 5, sl st in sc, 1 sc in same point, ch 7, p, ch 3, 2 sc in next 2d row, 3 sc in next, 2 sc in next. Repeat from * to end.

No. 61—INSERTION

Start here.

WIDTH—1¾ inches.

MATERIALS—Lily SIX CORD Mercerized Crochet Cotton, size 30.

Ch 36, dc in 9th st from hook, (ch 2, dc in next 3d st) 3 times, dc in next 6 sts, (ch 2, dc in next 3d st) 4 times (4 sps, 2 bls and 4 sps made). **ROW 2**—Ch 5, turn, dc in next dc, 2 sps, 4 bls and 3 sps. **ROW 3**—Ch 5, turn, dc in next dc, 1 sp, 2 bls, ch 6, 3 tr in 6th st from hook, holding the last loop of each tr on hook, thread over and pull thru all 4 loops on hook at once (a Cluster), ch 7, a Cluster in 6th st from hook, ch 1, sk 5 dc, 2 bls and 2 sps. **ROW 4**—Turn, 1 sp, 2 bls, ch 6, a Cluster, ch 1, 3 dc in 1-ch between next 2 Clusters, ch 6, a Cluster, ch 1, sk 3 dc, 2 bls, 1 sp. **ROW 5**—Turn, 1 sp, 1 bl, ch 6, a Cluster, ch 1, dc between next Cluster and dc, ch 1, 3 dc in center dc, ch 1, sk next dc, dc over next 1-ch, ch 6, a Cluster, ch 1, sk 3 dc, 1 bl, 1 sp. Turn, 1 sp, 1 bl. Ch 3, turn, 1 bl, 1 sp. Turn, 1 sp, 1 bl, ch 6, a Cluster, ch 1, sk next Cluster, sc in next dc, sc over next 1-ch, sc in 3 center dc, sc over next 1-ch, sc in next dc, ch 6, a Cluster, ch 7, 1 bl, 1 sp. Ch 5, turn, dc in next 3 dc, sk 2 sts of 7-ch, sl st in next 4 sts, turn, dc in last 3 dc, 1 sp. **ROW 9**—Turn, 1 sp, 1 bl, ch 8, a Cluster in 6th st from hook, sk next Cluster, dc in next sc, ch 1, sk 1 sc, (dc in next 3 sc) made into a Cluster, ch 1, dc in next 2d sc, ch 6, a Cluster, ch 3, sk next Cluster, 1 bl, 1 sp. **ROW 10**—Turn, 1 sp, 1 bl, 3 dc over next 3-ch, ch 8, a Cluster in 6th st from hook, ch 1, sk next Cluster, (dc in next 1-ch, dc in center Cluster, dc in next 1-ch) made into a Cluster, ch 6, a Cluster, ch 3, sk next Cluster, 2 bls, 1 sp. **ROW 11**—Turn, 2 sps, 2 bls, ch 5, sk 2 Clusters, 2 bls, 2 sps. **ROW 12**—Turn, 3 sps, 4 bls, 3 sps. **ROW 13**—Turn, 4 sps, 2 bls, 4 sps. Repeat from Row 2 for desired length.

A — For Size 70 . . . use No. 14 Steel Hook

B — For Size 60 . . . use No. 13 Steel Hook

C — For Size 50 . . . use No. 12 Steel Hook

D — For Size 40 . . . use No. 11 Steel Hook

E — For Size 30 . . . use No. 10 Steel Hook

One Edging, Many Sizes

On this page we demonstrate how any edging can be varied in size by changing the crochet cotton. The variations are shown in actual size, with specifications under each edging.

Starting at one long side, make a chain slightly longer than length desired. **1st row:** Dc in 8th ch from hook, * ch 2, skip next 2 ch, dc in next ch. Repeat from * across, having a number of sps divisible by 6. Ch 3, turn. **2nd row:** Sc in first sp, * ch 3, skip next sp, in next sp make (tr, ch 1) 7 times and tr; ch 3, skip next sp, sc in next sp, (ch 3, sc in next sp) twice. Repeat from * across, ending with sc in last sp. Ch 3, turn. **3rd row:** Sc in first loop, * (ch 3, sc in next ch-1 sp) 7 times; ch 3, skip next sp, sc in next loop, ch 3, sc in next loop. Repeat from * across, ending with sc in last loop. Ch 3, turn. **4th row:** Skip first sp, sc in next loop, * (ch 5, sc in 4th ch from hook—picot made—ch 2, sc in next loop) 5 times; (ch 3, skip next sp, sc in next loop) twice. Repeat from * across, ending with sc in last loop. Break off.

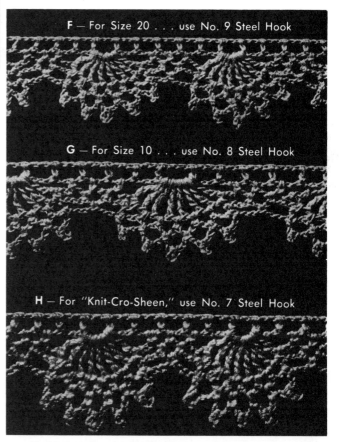

F — For Size 20 . . . use No. 9 Steel Hook

G — For Size 10 . . . use No. 8 Steel Hook

H — For "Knit-Cro-Sheen," use No. 7 Steel Hook

Simple Crochet Stitches

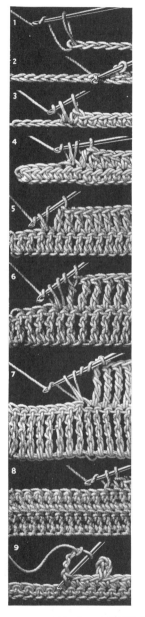

No. 1—Chain Stitch (CH) Form a loop on thread insert hook on loop and pull thread through tightening threads. Thread over hook and pull through last chain made. Continue chains for length desired.

No. 2—Slip Stitch (SL ST) Make a chain the desired length. Skip one chain, * insert hook in next chain, thread over hook and pull through stitch and loop on hook. Repeat from *. This stitch is used in joining and whenever an invisible stitch is required.

No. 3—Single Crochet (S C) Chain for desired length, skip 1 ch, * insert hook in next ch, thread over hook and pull through ch. There are now 2 loops on hook, thread over hook and pull through both loops, repeat from *. For succeeding rows of s c, ch 1, turn insert hook in top of next st taking up both threads and continue same as first row.

No. 4—Short Double Crochet (S D C) Ch for desired length thread over hook, insert hook in 3rd st from hook, draw thread through (3 loops on hook), thread over and draw through all three loops on hook. For succeeding rows, ch 2, turn.

No. 5—Double Crochet (D C) Ch for desired length, thread over hook, insert hook in 4th st from hook, draw thread through (3 loops on hook) thread over hook and pull through 2 loops thread over hook and pull through 2 loops. Succeeding rows, ch 3, turn and work next d c in 2nd d c of previous row. The ch 3 counts as 1 d c.

No. 6—Treble Crochet (TR C) Ch for desired length, thread over hook twice insert hook in 5th ch from hook draw thread through (4 loops on hook) thread over hook pull through 2 loops thread over, pull through 2 loops, thread over, pull through 2 loops. For succeeding rows ch 4, turn and work next tr c in 2nd tr c of previous row. The ch 4 counts as 1 tr c.

No. 7—Double Treble Crochet (D TR C) Ch for desired length thread over hook 3 times insert in 6th ch from hook (5 loops on hook) and work off 2 loops at a time same as tr c. For succeeding rows ch 5 turn and work next d tr c in 2nd d tr c of previous row. The ch 5 counts as 1 d tr c.

No. 8—Rib Stitch. Work this same as single crochet but insert hook in back loop of stitch only. This is sometimes called the slipper stitch.

No. 9—Picot (P) There are two methods of working the picot. (A) Work a single crochet in the foundation, ch 3 or 4 sts depending on the length of picot desired, sl st in top of s c made. (B) Work an s c, ch 3 or 4 for picot and s c in same space. Work as many single crochets between picots as desired.

No. 10—Open or Filet Mesh (O M.) When worked on a chain work the first d c in 8th ch from hook * ch 2, skip 2 sts, 1 d c in next st, repeat from *. Succeeding rows ch 5 to turn, d c in d c, ch 2, d c in next d c, repeat from *.

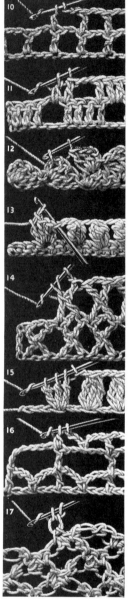

No. 11—Block or Solid Mesh (S M) Four double crochets form 1 solid mesh and 3 d c are required for each additional solid mesh. Open mesh and solid mesh are used in Filet Crochet.

No. 12—Slanting Shell St. Ch for desired length, work 2 d c in 4th st from hook, skip 3 sts, sl st in next st, * ch 3, 2 d c in same st with sl st, skip 3 sts, sl st in next st. Repeat from *. **2nd Row.** Ch 3, turn 2 d c in sl st, sl st in 3 ch loop of shell in previous row, * ch 3, 2 d c in same space, sl st in next shell, repeat from *.

No. 13—Bean or Pop Corn Stitch. Work 3 d c in same space, drop loop from hook insert hook in first d c made and draw loop through, ch 1 to tighten st.

No. 14—Cross Treble Crochet. Ch for desired length, thread over twice, insert in 5th st from hook, * work off two loops, thread over, skip 2 sts, insert in next st and work off all loops on needle 2 at a time, ch 2, d c in center to complete cross. Thread over twice, insert in next st and repeat from *.

No. 15—Cluster Stitch. Work 3 or 4 tr c in same st always retaining the last loop of each tr c on needle, thread over and pull through all loops on needle.

No. 16—Lacet St. Ch for desired length, work 1 s c in 10th st from hook, ch 3 skip 2 sts, 1 d c in next st, * ch 3, skip 2 sts, 1 s c in next st, ch 3, skip 2 sts 1 d c in next st, repeat from * to end of row, 2nd row, d c in d c, ch 5 d c in next d c.

No. 17—Knot Stitch (Sometimes Called Lovers Knot St.) Ch for desired length, * draw a ¼ inch loop on hook, thread over and pull through ch, s c in single loop of st, draw another ¼ inch loop, s c into loop, skip 4 sts, s c in next st, repeat from *. To turn make ⅜" knots, * s c in loop at right of s c and s c in loop at left of s c of previous row, 2 knot sts and repeat from *.

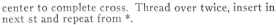

Metric Conversion Chart

CONVERTING INCHES TO CENTIMETERS AND YARDS TO METERS

mm — millimeters   cm — centimeters   m — meters

INCHES INTO MILLIMETERS AND CENTIMETERS
(Slightly rounded off for convenience)

inches	mm		cm	inches	cm	inches	cm	inches	cm
⅛	3mm			5	12.5	21	53.5	38	96.5
¼	6mm			5½	14	22	56	39	99
⅜	10mm	or	1cm	6	15	23	58.5	40	101.5
½	13mm	or	1.3cm	7	18	24	61	41	104
⅝	15mm	or	1.5cm	8	20.5	25	63.5	42	106.5
¾	20mm	or	2cm	9	23	26	66	43	109
⅞	22mm	or	2.2cm	10	25.5	27	68.5	44	112
1	25mm	or	2.5cm	11	28	28	71	45	114.5
1¼	32mm	or	3.2cm	12	30.5	29	73.5	46	117
1½	38mm	or	3.8cm	13	33	30	76	47	119.5
1¾	45mm	or	4.5cm	14	35.5	31	79	48	122
2	50mm	or	5cm	15	38	32	81.5	49	124.5
2½	65mm	or	6.5cm	16	40.5	33	84	50	127
3	75mm	or	7.5cm	17	43	34	86.5		
3½	90mm	or	9cm	18	46	35	89		
4	100mm	or	10cm	19	48.5	36	91.5		
4½	115mm	or	11.5cm	20	51	37	94		

YARDS TO METERS
(Slightly rounded off for convenience)

yards	meters	yards	meters	yards	meters	yards	meters	yards	meters
⅛	0.15	2⅛	1.95	4⅛	3.80	6⅛	5.60	8⅛	7.45
¼	0.25	2¼	2.10	4¼	3.90	6¼	5.75	8¼	7.55
⅜	0.35	2⅜	2.20	4⅜	4.00	6⅜	5.85	8⅜	7.70
½	0.50	2½	2.30	4½	4.15	6½	5.95	8½	7.80
⅝	0.60	2⅝	2.40	4⅝	4.25	6⅝	6.10	8⅝	7.90
¾	0.70	2¾	2.55	4¾	4.35	6¾	6.20	8¾	8.00
⅞	0.80	2⅞	2.65	4⅞	4.50	6⅞	6.30	8⅞	8.15
1	0.95	3	2.75	5	4.60	7	6.40	9	8.25
1⅛	1.05	3⅛	2.90	5⅛	4.70	7⅛	6.55	9⅛	8.35
1¼	1.15	3¼	3.00	5¼	4.80	7¼	6.65	9¼	8.50
1⅜	1.30	3⅜	3.10	5⅜	4.95	7⅜	6.75	9⅜	8.60
1½	1.40	3½	3.20	5½	5.05	7½	6.90	9½	8.70
1⅝	1.50	3⅝	3.35	5⅝	5.15	7⅝	7.00	9⅝	8.80
1¾	1.60	3¾	3.45	5¾	5.30	7¾	7.10	9¾	8.95
1⅞	1.75	3⅞	3.55	5⅞	5.40	7⅞	7.20	9⅞	9.05
2	1.85	4	3.70	6	5.50	8	7.35	10	9.15

AVAILABLE FABRIC WIDTHS

25"	65cm	50"	127cm
27"	70cm	54"/56"	140cm
35"/36"	90cm	58"/60"	150cm
39"	100cm	68"/70"	175cm
44"/45"	115cm	72"	180cm
48"	122cm		

AVAILABLE ZIPPER LENGTHS

4"	10cm	10"	25cm	22"	55cm
5"	12cm	12"	30cm	24"	60cm
6"	15cm	14"	35cm	26"	65cm
7"	18cm	16"	40cm	28"	70cm
8"	20cm	18"	45cm	30"	75cm
9"	22cm	20"	50cm		